Genealogy n

Jacobien Beeker

Copyright © 2016 Jacobien Beeker

All rights reserved.

ISBN-10: 1523726032
ISBN-13: 978-1523726035

This book belongs to:

Contents

Chapter 1: Ancestor data sheets — Page 7

Chapter 2: Alternate spellings of names — Page 389

Chapter 3: Places — Page 395

Chapter 4: Places of Worship — Page 403

Chapter 5: General notes — Page 411

Chapter 6: Genealogical table (Ahnentafel) — Page 421

Chapter 7: Research log — Page 431

Chapter 8: To-do list — Page 441

Chapter 9: Archives & Genealogical organizations — Page 449

Chapter 10: File index — Page 457

Chapter 11: Index of ancestors' names — Page 463

Chapter 1: Ancestors

This chapter contains 127 ancestor data sheets. Each sheet consists of 3 pages.
On the first two pages you can fill in all the basic information about the ancestor, such as name, date of birth, place of birth, date of death, children, spouses and so forth.
On the third page there is room for a short biography.

At the top of the first page you write the person's full name and his/her number in the genealogical table (Chapter 6). For example: Elisabeth Johanna de Witt, number 15 (great-grandmother)

You'll find after the name of a subject's relative (e.g. child, brother, sister, spouse) a column titled 'Page'. Here you can fill in the page number of the data sheet of that particular ancestor.

Note: Chapter 11 offers you a way to index all of the ancestors named in Chapter 1.

1. Full name: **Genealogical table number:**

Surname	
First name	
Gender	
Date of birth	
Place of birth	
Christened	
Occupation	
Date of death	
Place of death	
Date of burial	
Place of burial	

Parents

	Name	Page
Father		
Mother		

Marriage

Name	Place of marriage	Date	Page

Marriages ending in widowhood or divorce

Name	Widowhood or divorce	Date	Page

Children

	Name	Name of co-parent	Page
1			
2			
3			
4			
5			
6			
7			
8			
9			
10			
11			
12			

Brothers & Sisters

	Name	Date of birth	Page
1			
2			
3			
4			
5			
6			
7			
8			
9			
10			
11			
12			

Biography

Here you can write a description of the person's life. For example, you can describe the person's education, work, life events, personality, and the places he/she lived.

2. **Full name:**   **Genealogical table number:**

Surname	
First name	
Gender	
Date of birth	
Place of birth	
Christened	
Occupation	
Date of death	
Place of death	
Date of burial	
Place of burial	

Parents

	Name	Page
Father		
Mother		

Marriage

Name	Place of marriage	Date	Page

Marriages ending in widowhood or divorce

Name	Widowhood or divorce	Date	Page

Children

	Name	Name of co-parent	Page
1			
2			
3			
4			
5			
6			
7			
8			
9			
10			
11			
12			

Brothers & Sisters

	Name	Date of birth	Page
1			
2			
3			
4			
5			
6			
7			
8			
9			
10			
11			
12			

Biography

Here you can write a description of the person's life. For example, you can describe the person's education, work, life events, personality, and the places he/she lived.

3. **Full name:**   **Genealogical table number:**

Surname	
First name	
Gender	
Date of birth	
Place of birth	
Christened	
Occupation	
Date of death	
Place of death	
Date of burial	
Place of burial	

Parents

	Name	Page
Father		
Mother		

Marriage

Name	Place of marriage	Date	Page

Marriages ending in widowhood or divorce

Name	Widowhood or divorce	Date	Page

Children

	Name	Name of co-parent	Page
1			
2			
3			
4			
5			
6			
7			
8			
9			
10			
11			
12			

Brothers & Sisters

	Name	Date of birth	Page
1			
2			
3			
4			
5			
6			
7			
8			
9			
10			
11			
12			

Biography

Here you can write a description of the person's life. For example, you can describe the person's education, work, life events, personality, and the places he/she lived.

4. Full name: Genealogical table number:

Surname	
First name	
Gender	
Date of birth	
Place of birth	
Christened	
Occupation	
Date of death	
Place of death	
Date of burial	
Place of burial	

Parents

	Name	Page
Father		
Mother		

Marriage

Name	Place of marriage	Date	Page

Marriages ending in widowhood or divorce

Name	Widowhood or divorce	Date	Page

Children

	Name	Name of co-parent	Page
1			
2			
3			
4			
5			
6			
7			
8			
9			
10			
11			
12			

Brothers & Sisters

	Name	Date of birth	Page
1			
2			
3			
4			
5			
6			
7			
8			
9			
10			
11			
12			

Biography

Here you can write a description of the person's life. For example, you can describe the person's education, work, life events, personality, and the places he/she lived.

5. Full name: **Genealogical table number:**

Surname	
First name	
Gender	
Date of birth	
Place of birth	
Christened	
Occupation	
Date of death	
Place of death	
Date of burial	
Place of burial	

Parents

	Name	Page
Father		
Mother		

Marriage

Name	Place of marriage	Date	Page

Marriages ending in widowhood or divorce

Name	Widowhood or divorce	Date	Page

Children

	Name	Name of co-parent	Page
1			
2			
3			
4			
5			
6			
7			
8			
9			
10			
11			
12			

Brothers & Sisters

	Name	Date of birth	Page
1			
2			
3			
4			
5			
6			
7			
8			
9			
10			
11			
12			

Biography

Here you can write a description of the person's life. For example, you can describe the person's education, work, life events, personality, and the places he/she lived.

6. Full name: Genealogical table number:

Surname	
First name	
Gender	
Date of birth	
Place of birth	
Christened	
Occupation	
Date of death	
Place of death	
Date of burial	
Place of burial	

Parents

	Name	Page
Father		
Mother		

Marriage

Name	Place of marriage	Date	Page

Marriages ending in widowhood or divorce

Name	Widowhood or divorce	Date	Page

Children

	Name	Name of co-parent	Page
1			
2			
3			
4			
5			
6			
7			
8			
9			
10			
11			
12			

Brothers & Sisters

	Name	Date of birth	Page
1			
2			
3			
4			
5			
6			
7			
8			
9			
10			
11			
12			

Biography

Here you can write a description of the person's life. For example, you can describe the person's education, work, life events, personality, and the places he/she lived.

7. Full name: Genealogical table number:

Surname	
First name	
Gender	
Date of birth	
Place of birth	
Christened	
Occupation	
Date of death	
Place of death	
Date of burial	
Place of burial	

Parents

	Name	Page
Father		
Mother		

Marriage

Name	Place of marriage	Date	Page

Marriages ending in widowhood or divorce

Name	Widowhood or divorce	Date	Page

Children

	Name	Name of co-parent	Page
1			
2			
3			
4			
5			
6			
7			
8			
9			
10			
11			
12			

Brothers & Sisters

	Name	Date of birth	Page
1			
2			
3			
4			
5			
6			
7			
8			
9			
10			
11			
12			

Biography

Here you can write a description of the person's life. For example, you can describe the person's education, work, life events, personality, and the places he/she lived.

8. Full name: Genealogical table number:

Surname	
First name	
Gender	
Date of birth	
Place of birth	
Christened	
Occupation	
Date of death	
Place of death	
Date of burial	
Place of burial	

Parents

	Name	Page
Father		
Mother		

Marriage

Name	Place of marriage	Date	Page

Marriages ending in widowhood or divorce

Name	Widowhood or divorce	Date	Page

Children

	Name	Name of co-parent	Page
1			
2			
3			
4			
5			
6			
7			
8			
9			
10			
11			
12			

Brothers & Sisters

	Name	Date of birth	Page
1			
2			
3			
4			
5			
6			
7			
8			
9			
10			
11			
12			

Biography

Here you can write a description of the person's life. For example, you can describe the person's education, work, life events, personality, and the places he/she lived.

9. **Full name:** **Genealogical table number:**

Surname	
First name	
Gender	
Date of birth	
Place of birth	
Christened	
Occupation	
Date of death	
Place of death	
Date of burial	
Place of burial	

Parents

	Name	Page
Father		
Mother		

Marriage

Name	Place of marriage	Date	Page

Marriages ending in widowhood or divorce

Name	Widowhood or divorce	Date	Page

Children

	Name	Name of co-parent	Page
1			
2			
3			
4			
5			
6			
7			
8			
9			
10			
11			
12			

Brothers & Sisters

	Name	Date of birth	Page
1			
2			
3			
4			
5			
6			
7			
8			
9			
10			
11			
12			

Biography

Here you can write a description of the person's life. For example, you can describe the person's education, work, life events, personality, and the places he/she lived.

10. Full name: Genealogical table number:

Surname	
First name	
Gender	
Date of birth	
Place of birth	
Christened	
Occupation	
Date of death	
Place of death	
Date of burial	
Place of burial	

Parents

	Name	Page
Father		
Mother		

Marriage

Name	Place of marriage	Date	Page

Marriages ending in widowhood or divorce

Name	Widowhood or divorce	Date	Page

Children

	Name	Name of co-parent	Page
1			
2			
3			
4			
5			
6			
7			
8			
9			
10			
11			
12			

Brothers & Sisters

	Name	Date of birth	Page
1			
2			
3			
4			
5			
6			
7			
8			
9			
10			
11			
12			

Biography

Here you can write a description of the person's life. For example, you can describe the person's education, work, life events, personality, and the places he/she lived.

11. Full name: Genealogical table number:

Surname	
First name	
Gender	
Date of birth	
Place of birth	
Christened	
Occupation	
Date of death	
Place of death	
Date of burial	
Place of burial	

Parents

	Name	Page
Father		
Mother		

Marriage

Name	Place of marriage	Date	Page

Marriages ending in widowhood or divorce

Name	Widowhood or divorce	Date	Page

Children

	Name	Name of co-parent	Page
1			
2			
3			
4			
5			
6			
7			
8			
9			
10			
11			
12			

Brothers & Sisters

	Name	Date of birth	Page
1			
2			
3			
4			
5			
6			
7			
8			
9			
10			
11			
12			

Biography

Here you can write a description of the person's life. For example, you can describe the person's education, work, life events, personality, and the places he/she lived.

12. Full name: **Genealogical table number:**

Surname	
First name	
Gender	
Date of birth	
Place of birth	
Christened	
Occupation	
Date of death	
Place of death	
Date of burial	
Place of burial	

Parents

	Name	Page
Father		
Mother		

Marriage

Name	Place of marriage	Date	Page

Marriages ending in widowhood or divorce

Name	Widowhood or divorce	Date	Page

Children

	Name	Name of co-parent	Page
1			
2			
3			
4			
5			
6			
7			
8			
9			
10			
11			
12			

Brothers & Sisters

	Name	Date of birth	Page
1			
2			
3			
4			
5			
6			
7			
8			
9			
10			
11			
12			

Biography

Here you can write a description of the person's life. For example, you can describe the person's education, work, life events, personality, and the places he/she lived.

13. Full name: **Genealogical table number:**

Surname	
First name	
Gender	
Date of birth	
Place of birth	
Christened	
Occupation	
Date of death	
Place of death	
Date of burial	
Place of burial	

Parents

	Name	Page
Father		
Mother		

Marriage

Name	Place of marriage	Date	Page

Marriages ending in widowhood or divorce

Name	Widowhood or divorce	Date	Page

Children

	Name	Name of co-parent	Page
1			
2			
3			
4			
5			
6			
7			
8			
9			
10			
11			
12			

Brothers & Sisters

	Name	Date of birth	Page
1			
2			
3			
4			
5			
6			
7			
8			
9			
10			
11			
12			

Biography

Here you can write a description of the person's life. For example, you can describe the person's education, work, life events, personality, and the places he/she lived.

14. Full name: Genealogical table number:

Surname	
First name	
Gender	
Date of birth	
Place of birth	
Christened	
Occupation	
Date of death	
Place of death	
Date of burial	
Place of burial	

Parents

	Name	Page
Father		
Mother		

Marriage

Name	Place of marriage	Date	Page

Marriages ending in widowhood or divorce

Name	Widowhood or divorce	Date	Page

Children

	Name	Name of co-parent	Page
1			
2			
3			
4			
5			
6			
7			
8			
9			
10			
11			
12			

Brothers & Sisters

	Name	Date of birth	Page
1			
2			
3			
4			
5			
6			
7			
8			
9			
10			
11			
12			

Biography

Here you can write a description of the person's life. For example, you can describe the person's education, work, life events, personality, and the places he/she lived.

15. Full name: **Genealogical table number:**

Surname	
First name	
Gender	
Date of birth	
Place of birth	
Christened	
Occupation	
Date of death	
Place of death	
Date of burial	
Place of burial	

Parents

	Name	Page
Father		
Mother		

Marriage

Name	Place of marriage	Date	Page

Marriages ending in widowhood or divorce

Name	Widowhood or divorce	Date	Page

Children

	Name	Name of co-parent	Page
1			
2			
3			
4			
5			
6			
7			
8			
9			
10			
11			
12			

Brothers & Sisters

	Name	Date of birth	Page
1			
2			
3			
4			
5			
6			
7			
8			
9			
10			
11			
12			

Biography

Here you can write a description of the person's life. For example, you can describe the person's education, work, life events, personality, and the places he/she lived.

16. Full name: Genealogical table number:

Surname	
First name	
Gender	
Date of birth	
Place of birth	
Christened	
Occupation	
Date of death	
Place of death	
Date of burial	
Place of burial	

Parents

	Name	Page
Father		
Mother		

Marriage

Name	Place of marriage	Date	Page

Marriages ending in widowhood or divorce

Name	Widowhood or divorce	Date	Page

Children

	Name	Name of co-parent	Page
1			
2			
3			
4			
5			
6			
7			
8			
9			
10			
11			
12			

Brothers & Sisters

	Name	Date of birth	Page
1			
2			
3			
4			
5			
6			
7			
8			
9			
10			
11			
12			

Biography

Here you can write a description of the person's life. For example, you can describe the person's education, work, life events, personality, and the places he/she lived.

17. Full name: Genealogical table number:

Surname	
First name	
Gender	
Date of birth	
Place of birth	
Christened	
Occupation	
Date of death	
Place of death	
Date of burial	
Place of burial	

Parents

	Name	Page
Father		
Mother		

Marriage

Name	Place of marriage	Date	Page

Marriages ending in widowhood or divorce

Name	Widowhood or divorce	Date	Page

Children

	Name	Name of co-parent	Page
1			
2			
3			
4			
5			
6			
7			
8			
9			
10			
11			
12			

Brothers & Sisters

	Name	Date of birth	Page
1			
2			
3			
4			
5			
6			
7			
8			
9			
10			
11			
12			

Biography

Here you can write a description of the person's life. For example, you can describe the person's education, work, life events, personality, and the places he/she lived.

18. Full name: Genealogical table number:

Surname	
First name	
Gender	
Date of birth	
Place of birth	
Christened	
Occupation	
Date of death	
Place of death	
Date of burial	
Place of burial	

Parents

	Name	Page
Father		
Mother		

Marriage

Name	Place of marriage	Date	Page

Marriages ending in widowhood or divorce

Name	Widowhood or divorce	Date	Page

Children

	Name	Name of co-parent	Page
1			
2			
3			
4			
5			
6			
7			
8			
9			
10			
11			
12			

Brothers & Sisters

	Name	Date of birth	Page
1			
2			
3			
4			
5			
6			
7			
8			
9			
10			
11			
12			

Biography

Here you can write a description of the person's life. For example, you can describe the person's education, work, life events, personality, and the places he/she lived.

19. Full name: **Genealogical table number:**

Surname	
First name	
Gender	
Date of birth	
Place of birth	
Christened	
Occupation	
Date of death	
Place of death	
Date of burial	
Place of burial	

Parents

	Name	Page
Father		
Mother		

Marriage

Name	Place of marriage	Date	Page

Marriages ending in widowhood or divorce

Name	Widowhood or divorce	Date	Page

Children

	Name	Name of co-parent	Page
1			
2			
3			
4			
5			
6			
7			
8			
9			
10			
11			
12			

Brothers & Sisters

	Name	Date of birth	Page
1			
2			
3			
4			
5			
6			
7			
8			
9			
10			
11			
12			

Biography

Here you can write a description of the person's life. For example, you can describe the person's education, work, life events, personality, and the places he/she lived.

20. Full name: **Genealogical table number:**

Surname	
First name	
Gender	
Date of birth	
Place of birth	
Christened	
Occupation	
Date of death	
Place of death	
Date of burial	
Place of burial	

Parents

	Name	Page
Father		
Mother		

Marriage

Name	Place of marriage	Date	Page

Marriages ending in widowhood or divorce

Name	Widowhood or divorce	Date	Page

Children

	Name	Name of co-parent	Page
1			
2			
3			
4			
5			
6			
7			
8			
9			
10			
11			
12			

Brothers & Sisters

	Name	Date of birth	Page
1			
2			
3			
4			
5			
6			
7			
8			
9			
10			
11			
12			

Biography

Here you can write a description of the person's life. For example, you can describe the person's education, work, life events, personality, and the places he/she lived.

21. Full name: Genealogical table number:

Surname	
First name	
Gender	
Date of birth	
Place of birth	
Christened	
Occupation	
Date of death	
Place of death	
Date of burial	
Place of burial	

Parents

	Name	Page
Father		
Mother		

Marriage

Name	Place of marriage	Date	Page

Marriages ending in widowhood or divorce

Name	Widowhood or divorce	Date	Page

Children

	Name	Name of co-parent	Page
1			
2			
3			
4			
5			
6			
7			
8			
9			
10			
11			
12			

Brothers & Sisters

	Name	Date of birth	Page
1			
2			
3			
4			
5			
6			
7			
8			
9			
10			
11			
12			

Biography

Here you can write a description of the person's life. For example, you can describe the person's education, work, life events, personality, and the places he/she lived.

22. Full name: Genealogical table number:

Surname	
First name	
Gender	
Date of birth	
Place of birth	
Christened	
Occupation	
Date of death	
Place of death	
Date of burial	
Place of burial	

Parents

	Name	Page
Father		
Mother		

Marriage

Name	Place of marriage	Date	Page

Marriages ending in widowhood or divorce

Name	Widowhood or divorce	Date	Page

Children

	Name	Name of co-parent	Page
1			
2			
3			
4			
5			
6			
7			
8			
9			
10			
11			
12			

Brothers & Sisters

	Name	Date of birth	Page
1			
2			
3			
4			
5			
6			
7			
8			
9			
10			
11			
12			

Biography

Here you can write a description of the person's life. For example, you can describe the person's education, work, life events, personality, and the places he/she lived.

23. Full name: Genealogical table number:

Surname	
First name	
Gender	
Date of birth	
Place of birth	
Christened	
Occupation	
Date of death	
Place of death	
Date of burial	
Place of burial	

Parents

	Name	Page
Father		
Mother		

Marriage

Name	Place of marriage	Date	Page

Marriages ending in widowhood or divorce

Name	Widowhood or divorce	Date	Page

Children

	Name	Name of co-parent	Page
1			
2			
3			
4			
5			
6			
7			
8			
9			
10			
11			
12			

Brothers & Sisters

	Name	Date of birth	Page
1			
2			
3			
4			
5			
6			
7			
8			
9			
10			
11			
12			

Biography

Here you can write a description of the person's life. For example, you can describe the person's education, work, life events, personality, and the places he/she lived.

24. Full name: **Genealogical table number:**

Surname	
First name	
Gender	
Date of birth	
Place of birth	
Christened	
Occupation	
Date of death	
Place of death	
Date of burial	
Place of burial	

Parents

	Name	Page
Father		
Mother		

Marriage

Name	Place of marriage	Date	Page

Marriages ending in widowhood or divorce

Name	Widowhood or divorce	Date	Page

Children

	Name	Name of co-parent	Page
1			
2			
3			
4			
5			
6			
7			
8			
9			
10			
11			
12			

Brothers & Sisters

	Name	Date of birth	Page
1			
2			
3			
4			
5			
6			
7			
8			
9			
10			
11			
12			

Biography

Here you can write a description of the person's life. For example, you can describe the person's education, work, life events, personality, and the places he/she lived.

25. Full name: **Genealogical table number:**

Surname	
First name	
Gender	
Date of birth	
Place of birth	
Christened	
Occupation	
Date of death	
Place of death	
Date of burial	
Place of burial	

Parents

	Name	Page
Father		
Mother		

Marriage

Name	Place of marriage	Date	Page

Marriages ending in widowhood or divorce

Name	Widowhood or divorce	Date	Page

Children

	Name	Name of co-parent	Page
1			
2			
3			
4			
5			
6			
7			
8			
9			
10			
11			
12			

Brothers & Sisters

	Name	Date of birth	Page
1			
2			
3			
4			
5			
6			
7			
8			
9			
10			
11			
12			

Biography

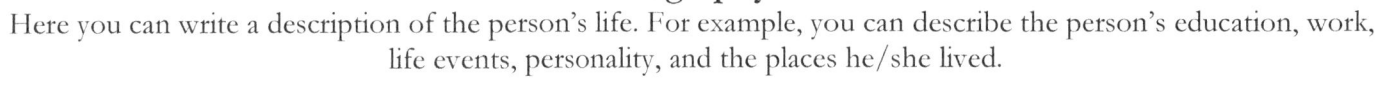

Here you can write a description of the person's life. For example, you can describe the person's education, work, life events, personality, and the places he/she lived.

26. Full name: Genealogical table number:

Surname	
First name	
Gender	
Date of birth	
Place of birth	
Christened	
Occupation	
Date of death	
Place of death	
Date of burial	
Place of burial	

Parents

	Name	Page
Father		
Mother		

Marriage

Name	Place of marriage	Date	Page

Marriages ending in widowhood or divorce

Name	Widowhood or divorce	Date	Page

Children

	Name	Name of co-parent	Page
1			
2			
3			
4			
5			
6			
7			
8			
9			
10			
11			
12			

Brothers & Sisters

	Name	Date of birth	Page
1			
2			
3			
4			
5			
6			
7			
8			
9			
10			
11			
12			

Biography

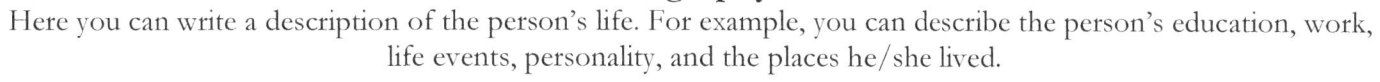

Here you can write a description of the person's life. For example, you can describe the person's education, work, life events, personality, and the places he/she lived.

27. Full name: Genealogical table number:

Surname	
First name	
Gender	
Date of birth	
Place of birth	
Christened	
Occupation	
Date of death	
Place of death	
Date of burial	
Place of burial	

Parents

	Name	Page
Father		
Mother		

Marriage

Name	Place of marriage	Date	Page

Marriages ending in widowhood or divorce

Name	Widowhood or divorce	Date	Page

Children

	Name	Name of co-parent	Page
1			
2			
3			
4			
5			
6			
7			
8			
9			
10			
11			
12			

Brothers & Sisters

	Name	Date of birth	Page
1			
2			
3			
4			
5			
6			
7			
8			
9			
10			
11			
12			

Biography

Here you can write a description of the person's life. For example, you can describe the person's education, work, life events, personality, and the places he/she lived.

28. Full name: Genealogical table number:

Surname	
First name	
Gender	
Date of birth	
Place of birth	
Christened	
Occupation	
Date of death	
Place of death	
Date of burial	
Place of burial	

Parents

	Name	Page
Father		
Mother		

Marriage

Name	Place of marriage	Date	Page

Marriages ending in widowhood or divorce

Name	Widowhood or divorce	Date	Page

Children

	Name	Name of co-parent	Page
1			
2			
3			
4			
5			
6			
7			
8			
9			
10			
11			
12			

Brothers & Sisters

	Name	Date of birth	Page
1			
2			
3			
4			
5			
6			
7			
8			
9			
10			
11			
12			

Biography

Here you can write a description of the person's life. For example, you can describe the person's education, work, life events, personality, and the places he/she lived.

29. Full name: Genealogical table number:

Surname	
First name	
Gender	
Date of birth	
Place of birth	
Christened	
Occupation	
Date of death	
Place of death	
Date of burial	
Place of burial	

Parents

	Name	Page
Father		
Mother		

Marriage

Name	Place of marriage	Date	Page

Marriages ending in widowhood or divorce

Name	Widowhood or divorce	Date	Page

Children

	Name	Name of co-parent	Page
1			
2			
3			
4			
5			
6			
7			
8			
9			
10			
11			
12			

Brothers & Sisters

	Name	Date of birth	Page
1			
2			
3			
4			
5			
6			
7			
8			
9			
10			
11			
12			

Biography

Here you can write a description of the person's life. For example, you can describe the person's education, work, life events, personality, and the places he/she lived.

30. Full name: **Genealogical table number:**

Surname	
First name	
Gender	
Date of birth	
Place of birth	
Christened	
Occupation	
Date of death	
Place of death	
Date of burial	
Place of burial	

Parents

	Name	Page
Father		
Mother		

Marriage

Name	Place of marriage	Date	Page

Marriages ending in widowhood or divorce

Name	Widowhood or divorce	Date	Page

Children

	Name	Name of co-parent	Page
1			
2			
3			
4			
5			
6			
7			
8			
9			
10			
11			
12			

Brothers & Sisters

	Name	Date of birth	Page
1			
2			
3			
4			
5			
6			
7			
8			
9			
10			
11			
12			

Biography

Here you can write a description of the person's life. For example, you can describe the person's education, work, life events, personality, and the places he/she lived.

31. Full name: Genealogical table number:

Surname	
First name	
Gender	
Date of birth	
Place of birth	
Christened	
Occupation	
Date of death	
Place of death	
Date of burial	
Place of burial	

Parents

	Name	Page
Father		
Mother		

Marriage

Name	Place of marriage	Date	Page

Marriages ending in widowhood or divorce

Name	Widowhood or divorce	Date	Page

Children

	Name	Name of co-parent	Page
1			
2			
3			
4			
5			
6			
7			
8			
9			
10			
11			
12			

Brothers & Sisters

	Name	Date of birth	Page
1			
2			
3			
4			
5			
6			
7			
8			
9			
10			
11			
12			

Biography

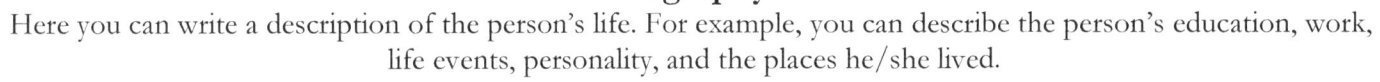

Here you can write a description of the person's life. For example, you can describe the person's education, work, life events, personality, and the places he/she lived.

32. Full name: **Genealogical table number:**

Surname	
First name	
Gender	
Date of birth	
Place of birth	
Christened	
Occupation	
Date of death	
Place of death	
Date of burial	
Place of burial	

Parents

	Name	Page
Father		
Mother		

Marriage

Name	Place of marriage	Date	Page

Marriages ending in widowhood or divorce

Name	Widowhood or divorce	Date	Page

Children

	Name	Name of co-parent	Page
1			
2			
3			
4			
5			
6			
7			
8			
9			
10			
11			
12			

Brothers & Sisters

	Name	Date of birth	Page
1			
2			
3			
4			
5			
6			
7			
8			
9			
10			
11			
12			

Biography

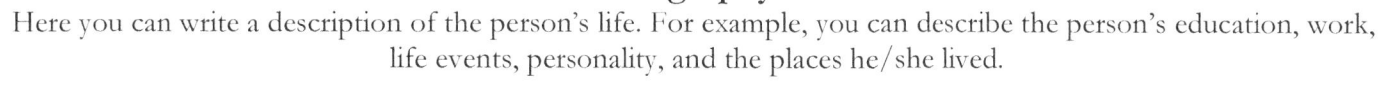

Here you can write a description of the person's life. For example, you can describe the person's education, work, life events, personality, and the places he/she lived.

33. Full name: **Genealogical table number:**

Surname	
First name	
Gender	
Date of birth	
Place of birth	
Christened	
Occupation	
Date of death	
Place of death	
Date of burial	
Place of burial	

Parents

	Name	Page
Father		
Mother		

Marriage

Name	Place of marriage	Date	Page

Marriages ending in widowhood or divorce

Name	Widowhood or divorce	Date	Page

Children

	Name	Name of co-parent	Page
1			
2			
3			
4			
5			
6			
7			
8			
9			
10			
11			
12			

Brothers & Sisters

	Name	Date of birth	Page
1			
2			
3			
4			
5			
6			
7			
8			
9			
10			
11			
12			

Biography

Here you can write a description of the person's life. For example, you can describe the person's education, work, life events, personality, and the places he/she lived.

34. Full name: Genealogical table number:

Surname	
First name	
Gender	
Date of birth	
Place of birth	
Christened	
Occupation	
Date of death	
Place of death	
Date of burial	
Place of burial	

Parents

	Name	Page
Father		
Mother		

Marriage

Name	Place of marriage	Date	Page

Marriages ending in widowhood or divorce

Name	Widowhood or divorce	Date	Page

Children

	Name	Name of co-parent	Page
1			
2			
3			
4			
5			
6			
7			
8			
9			
10			
11			
12			

Brothers & Sisters

	Name	Date of birth	Page
1			
2			
3			
4			
5			
6			
7			
8			
9			
10			
11			
12			

Biography

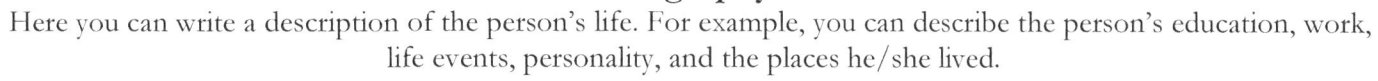

Here you can write a description of the person's life. For example, you can describe the person's education, work, life events, personality, and the places he/she lived.

35. Full name: Genealogical table number:

Surname	
First name	
Gender	
Date of birth	
Place of birth	
Christened	
Occupation	
Date of death	
Place of death	
Date of burial	
Place of burial	

Parents

	Name	Page
Father		
Mother		

Marriage

Name	Place of marriage	Date	Page

Marriages ending in widowhood or divorce

Name	Widowhood or divorce	Date	Page

Children

	Name	Name of co-parent	Page
1			
2			
3			
4			
5			
6			
7			
8			
9			
10			
11			
12			

Brothers & Sisters

	Name	Date of birth	Page
1			
2			
3			
4			
5			
6			
7			
8			
9			
10			
11			
12			

Biography

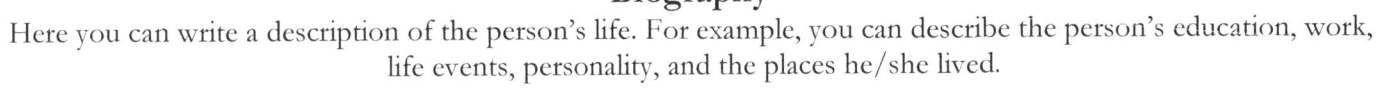

Here you can write a description of the person's life. For example, you can describe the person's education, work, life events, personality, and the places he/she lived.

36. Full name: Genealogical table number:

Surname	
First name	
Gender	
Date of birth	
Place of birth	
Christened	
Occupation	
Date of death	
Place of death	
Date of burial	
Place of burial	

Parents

	Name	Page
Father		
Mother		

Marriage

Name	Place of marriage	Date	Page

Marriages ending in widowhood or divorce

Name	Widowhood or divorce	Date	Page

Children

	Name	Name of co-parent	Page
1			
2			
3			
4			
5			
6			
7			
8			
9			
10			
11			
12			

Brothers & Sisters

	Name	Date of birth	Page
1			
2			
3			
4			
5			
6			
7			
8			
9			
10			
11			
12			

Biography

Here you can write a description of the person's life. For example, you can describe the person's education, work, life events, personality, and the places he/she lived.

37. Full name: Genealogical table number:

Surname	
First name	
Gender	
Date of birth	
Place of birth	
Christened	
Occupation	
Date of death	
Place of death	
Date of burial	
Place of burial	

Parents

	Name	Page
Father		
Mother		

Marriage

Name	Place of marriage	Date	Page

Marriages ending in widowhood or divorce

Name	Widowhood or divorce	Date	Page

Children

	Name	Name of co-parent	Page
1			
2			
3			
4			
5			
6			
7			
8			
9			
10			
11			
12			

Brothers & Sisters

	Name	Date of birth	Page
1			
2			
3			
4			
5			
6			
7			
8			
9			
10			
11			
12			

Biography

Here you can write a description of the person's life. For example, you can describe the person's education, work, life events, personality, and the places he/she lived.

38. Full name: Genealogical table number:

Surname	
First name	
Gender	
Date of birth	
Place of birth	
Christened	
Occupation	
Date of death	
Place of death	
Date of burial	
Place of burial	

Parents

	Name	Page
Father		
Mother		

Marriage

Name	Place of marriage	Date	Page

Marriages ending in widowhood or divorce

Name	Widowhood or divorce	Date	Page

Children

	Name	Name of co-parent	Page
1			
2			
3			
4			
5			
6			
7			
8			
9			
10			
11			
12			

Brothers & Sisters

	Name	Date of birth	Page
1			
2			
3			
4			
5			
6			
7			
8			
9			
10			
11			
12			

Biography

Here you can write a description of the person's life. For example, you can describe the person's education, work, life events, personality, and the places he/she lived.

39. Full name: Genealogical table number:

Surname	
First name	
Gender	
Date of birth	
Place of birth	
Christened	
Occupation	
Date of death	
Place of death	
Date of burial	
Place of burial	

Parents

	Name	Page
Father		
Mother		

Marriage

Name	Place of marriage	Date	Page

Marriages ending in widowhood or divorce

Name	Widowhood or divorce	Date	Page

Children

	Name	Name of co-parent	Page
1			
2			
3			
4			
5			
6			
7			
8			
9			
10			
11			
12			

Brothers & Sisters

	Name	Date of birth	Page
1			
2			
3			
4			
5			
6			
7			
8			
9			
10			
11			
12			

Biography

Here you can write a description of the person's life. For example, you can describe the person's education, work, life events, personality, and the places he/she lived.

40. Full name: Genealogical table number:

Surname	
First name	
Gender	
Date of birth	
Place of birth	
Christened	
Occupation	
Date of death	
Place of death	
Date of burial	
Place of burial	

Parents

	Name	Page
Father		
Mother		

Marriage

Name	Place of marriage	Date	Page

Marriages ending in widowhood or divorce

Name	Widowhood or divorce	Date	Page

Children

	Name	Name of co-parent	Page
1			
2			
3			
4			
5			
6			
7			
8			
9			
10			
11			
12			

Brothers & Sisters

	Name	Date of birth	Page
1			
2			
3			
4			
5			
6			
7			
8			
9			
10			
11			
12			

Biography

Here you can write a description of the person's life. For example, you can describe the person's education, work, life events, personality, and the places he/she lived.

41. Full name: Genealogical table number:

Surname	
First name	
Gender	
Date of birth	
Place of birth	
Christened	
Occupation	
Date of death	
Place of death	
Date of burial	
Place of burial	

Parents

	Name	Page
Father		
Mother		

Marriage

Name	Place of marriage	Date	Page

Marriages ending in widowhood or divorce

Name	Widowhood or divorce	Date	Page

Children

	Name	Name of co-parent	Page
1			
2			
3			
4			
5			
6			
7			
8			
9			
10			
11			
12			

Brothers & Sisters

	Name	Date of birth	Page
1			
2			
3			
4			
5			
6			
7			
8			
9			
10			
11			
12			

Biography

Here you can write a description of the person's life. For example, you can describe the person's education, work, life events, personality, and the places he/she lived.

42. Full name: Genealogical table number:

Surname	
First name	
Gender	
Date of birth	
Place of birth	
Christened	
Occupation	
Date of death	
Place of death	
Date of burial	
Place of burial	

Parents

	Name	Page
Father		
Mother		

Marriage

Name	Place of marriage	Date	Page

Marriages ending in widowhood or divorce

Name	Widowhood or divorce	Date	Page

Children

	Name	Name of co-parent	Page
1			
2			
3			
4			
5			
6			
7			
8			
9			
10			
11			
12			

Brothers & Sisters

	Name	Date of birth	Page
1			
2			
3			
4			
5			
6			
7			
8			
9			
10			
11			
12			

Biography

Here you can write a description of the person's life. For example, you can describe the person's education, work, life events, personality, and the places he/she lived.

43. Full name: Genealogical table number:

Surname	
First name	
Gender	
Date of birth	
Place of birth	
Christened	
Occupation	
Date of death	
Place of death	
Date of burial	
Place of burial	

Parents

	Name	Page
Father		
Mother		

Marriage

Name	Place of marriage	Date	Page

Marriages ending in widowhood or divorce

Name	Widowhood or divorce	Date	Page

Children

	Name	Name of co-parent	Page
1			
2			
3			
4			
5			
6			
7			
8			
9			
10			
11			
12			

Brothers & Sisters

	Name	Date of birth	Page
1			
2			
3			
4			
5			
6			
7			
8			
9			
10			
11			
12			

Biography

Here you can write a description of the person's life. For example, you can describe the person's education, work, life events, personality, and the places he/she lived.

44. **Full name:**   **Genealogical table number:**

Surname	
First name	
Gender	
Date of birth	
Place of birth	
Christened	
Occupation	
Date of death	
Place of death	
Date of burial	
Place of burial	

Parents

	Name	Page
Father		
Mother		

Marriage

Name	Place of marriage	Date	Page

Marriages ending in widowhood or divorce

Name	Widowhood or divorce	Date	Page

Children

	Name	Name of co-parent	Page
1			
2			
3			
4			
5			
6			
7			
8			
9			
10			
11			
12			

Brothers & Sisters

	Name	Date of birth	Page
1			
2			
3			
4			
5			
6			
7			
8			
9			
10			
11			
12			

Biography

Here you can write a description of the person's life. For example, you can describe the person's education, work, life events, personality, and the places he/she lived.

45. Full name: Genealogical table number:

Surname	
First name	
Gender	
Date of birth	
Place of birth	
Christened	
Occupation	
Date of death	
Place of death	
Date of burial	
Place of burial	

Parents

	Name	Page
Father		
Mother		

Marriage

Name	Place of marriage	Date	Page

Marriages ending in widowhood or divorce

Name	Widowhood or divorce	Date	Page

Children

	Name	Name of co-parent	Page
1			
2			
3			
4			
5			
6			
7			
8			
9			
10			
11			
12			

Brothers & Sisters

	Name	Date of birth	Page
1			
2			
3			
4			
5			
6			
7			
8			
9			
10			
11			
12			

Biography

Here you can write a description of the person's life. For example, you can describe the person's education, work, life events, personality, and the places he/she lived.

46. Full name: **Genealogical table number:**

Surname	
First name	
Gender	
Date of birth	
Place of birth	
Christened	
Occupation	
Date of death	
Place of death	
Date of burial	
Place of burial	

Parents

	Name	Page
Father		
Mother		

Marriage

Name	Place of marriage	Date	Page

Marriages ending in widowhood or divorce

Name	Widowhood or divorce	Date	Page

Children

	Name	Name of co-parent	Page
1			
2			
3			
4			
5			
6			
7			
8			
9			
10			
11			
12			

Brothers & Sisters

	Name	Date of birth	Page
1			
2			
3			
4			
5			
6			
7			
8			
9			
10			
11			
12			

Biography

Here you can write a description of the person's life. For example, you can describe the person's education, work, life events, personality, and the places he/she lived.

47. Full name: **Genealogical table number:**

Surname	
First name	
Gender	
Date of birth	
Place of birth	
Christened	
Occupation	
Date of death	
Place of death	
Date of burial	
Place of burial	

Parents

	Name	Page
Father		
Mother		

Marriage

Name	Place of marriage	Date	Page

Marriages ending in widowhood or divorce

Name	Widowhood or divorce	Date	Page

Children

	Name	Name of co-parent	Page
1			
2			
3			
4			
5			
6			
7			
8			
9			
10			
11			
12			

Brothers & Sisters

	Name	Date of birth	Page
1			
2			
3			
4			
5			
6			
7			
8			
9			
10			
11			
12			

Biography

Here you can write a description of the person's life. For example, you can describe the person's education, work, life events, personality, and the places he/she lived.

48. Full name: Genealogical table number:

Surname	
First name	
Gender	
Date of birth	
Place of birth	
Christened	
Occupation	
Date of death	
Place of death	
Date of burial	
Place of burial	

Parents

	Name	Page
Father		
Mother		

Marriage

Name	Place of marriage	Date	Page

Marriages ending in widowhood or divorce

Name	Widowhood or divorce	Date	Page

Children

	Name	Name of co-parent	Page
1			
2			
3			
4			
5			
6			
7			
8			
9			
10			
11			
12			

Brothers & Sisters

	Name	Date of birth	Page
1			
2			
3			
4			
5			
6			
7			
8			
9			
10			
11			
12			

Biography

Here you can write a description of the person's life. For example, you can describe the person's education, work, life events, personality, and the places he/she lived.

49. Full name: **Genealogical table number:**

Surname	
First name	
Gender	
Date of birth	
Place of birth	
Christened	
Occupation	
Date of death	
Place of death	
Date of burial	
Place of burial	

Parents

	Name	Page
Father		
Mother		

Marriage

Name	Place of marriage	Date	Page

Marriages ending in widowhood or divorce

Name	Widowhood or divorce	Date	Page

Children

	Name	Name of co-parent	Page
1			
2			
3			
4			
5			
6			
7			
8			
9			
10			
11			
12			

Brothers & Sisters

	Name	Date of birth	Page
1			
2			
3			
4			
5			
6			
7			
8			
9			
10			
11			
12			

Biography

Here you can write a description of the person's life. For example, you can describe the person's education, work, life events, personality, and the places he/she lived.

50. Full name: **Genealogical table number:**

Surname	
First name	
Gender	
Date of birth	
Place of birth	
Christened	
Occupation	
Date of death	
Place of death	
Date of burial	
Place of burial	

Parents

	Name	Page
Father		
Mother		

Marriage

Name	Place of marriage	Date	Page

Marriages ending in widowhood or divorce

Name	Widowhood or divorce	Date	Page

Children

	Name	Name of co-parent	Page
1			
2			
3			
4			
5			
6			
7			
8			
9			
10			
11			
12			

Brothers & Sisters

	Name	Date of birth	Page
1			
2			
3			
4			
5			
6			
7			
8			
9			
10			
11			
12			

Biography

Here you can write a description of the person's life. For example, you can describe the person's education, work, life events, personality, and the places he/she lived.

51. Full name: Genealogical table number:

Surname	
First name	
Gender	
Date of birth	
Place of birth	
Christened	
Occupation	
Date of death	
Place of death	
Date of burial	
Place of burial	

Parents

	Name	Page
Father		
Mother		

Marriage

Name	Place of marriage	Date	Page

Marriages ending in widowhood or divorce

Name	Widowhood or divorce	Date	Page

Children

	Name	Name of co-parent	Page
1			
2			
3			
4			
5			
6			
7			
8			
9			
10			
11			
12			

Brothers & Sisters

	Name	Date of birth	Page
1			
2			
3			
4			
5			
6			
7			
8			
9			
10			
11			
12			

Biography

Here you can write a description of the person's life. For example, you can describe the person's education, work, life events, personality, and the places he/she lived.

52. Full name: Genealogical table number:

Surname	
First name	
Gender	
Date of birth	
Place of birth	
Christened	
Occupation	
Date of death	
Place of death	
Date of burial	
Place of burial	

Parents

	Name	Page
Father		
Mother		

Marriage

Name	Place of marriage	Date	Page

Marriages ending in widowhood or divorce

Name	Widowhood or divorce	Date	Page

Children

	Name	Name of co-parent	Page
1			
2			
3			
4			
5			
6			
7			
8			
9			
10			
11			
12			

Brothers & Sisters

	Name	Date of birth	Page
1			
2			
3			
4			
5			
6			
7			
8			
9			
10			
11			
12			

Biography

Here you can write a description of the person's life. For example, you can describe the person's education, work, life events, personality, and the places he/she lived.

53. Full name: Genealogical table number:

Surname	
First name	
Gender	
Date of birth	
Place of birth	
Christened	
Occupation	
Date of death	
Place of death	
Date of burial	
Place of burial	

Parents

	Name	Page
Father		
Mother		

Marriage

Name	Place of marriage	Date	Page

Marriages ending in widowhood or divorce

Name	Widowhood or divorce	Date	Page

Children

	Name	Name of co-parent	Page
1			
2			
3			
4			
5			
6			
7			
8			
9			
10			
11			
12			

Brothers & Sisters

	Name	Date of birth	Page
1			
2			
3			
4			
5			
6			
7			
8			
9			
10			
11			
12			

Biography

Here you can write a description of the person's life. For example, you can describe the person's education, work, life events, personality, and the places he/she lived.

54. Full name: 　　　　　　　　　　　　　　　　　　**Genealogical table number:**

Surname	
First name	
Gender	
Date of birth	
Place of birth	
Christened	
Occupation	
Date of death	
Place of death	
Date of burial	
Place of burial	

Parents

	Name	Page
Father		
Mother		

Marriage

Name	Place of marriage	Date	Page

Marriages ending in widowhood or divorce

Name	Widowhood or divorce	Date	Page

Children

	Name	Name of co-parent	Page
1			
2			
3			
4			
5			
6			
7			
8			
9			
10			
11			
12			

Brothers & Sisters

	Name	Date of birth	Page
1			
2			
3			
4			
5			
6			
7			
8			
9			
10			
11			
12			

Biography

Here you can write a description of the person's life. For example, you can describe the person's education, work, life events, personality, and the places he/she lived.

55. **Full name:**   **Genealogical table number:**

Surname	
First name	
Gender	
Date of birth	
Place of birth	
Christened	
Occupation	
Date of death	
Place of death	
Date of burial	
Place of burial	

Parents

	Name	Page
Father		
Mother		

Marriage

Name	Place of marriage	Date	Page

Marriages ending in widowhood or divorce

Name	Widowhood or divorce	Date	Page

Children

	Name	Name of co-parent	Page
1			
2			
3			
4			
5			
6			
7			
8			
9			
10			
11			
12			

Brothers & Sisters

	Name	Date of birth	Page
1			
2			
3			
4			
5			
6			
7			
8			
9			
10			
11			
12			

Biography

Here you can write a description of the person's life. For example, you can describe the person's education, work, life events, personality, and the places he/she lived.

56. Full name: **Genealogical table number:**

Surname	
First name	
Gender	
Date of birth	
Place of birth	
Christened	
Occupation	
Date of death	
Place of death	
Date of burial	
Place of burial	

Parents

	Name	Page
Father		
Mother		

Marriage

Name	Place of marriage	Date	Page

Marriages ending in widowhood or divorce

Name	Widowhood or divorce	Date	Page

Children

	Name	Name of co-parent	Page
1			
2			
3			
4			
5			
6			
7			
8			
9			
10			
11			
12			

Brothers & Sisters

	Name	Date of birth	Page
1			
2			
3			
4			
5			
6			
7			
8			
9			
10			
11			
12			

Biography

Here you can write a description of the person's life. For example, you can describe the person's education, work, life events, personality, and the places he/she lived.

57. Full name: 　　　　　　　　　　　　　　　　**Genealogical table number:**

Surname	
First name	
Gender	
Date of birth	
Place of birth	
Christened	
Occupation	
Date of death	
Place of death	
Date of burial	
Place of burial	

Parents

	Name	Page
Father		
Mother		

Marriage

Name	Place of marriage	Date	Page

Marriages ending in widowhood or divorce

Name	Widowhood or divorce	Date	Page

Children

	Name	Name of co-parent	Page
1			
2			
3			
4			
5			
6			
7			
8			
9			
10			
11			
12			

Brothers & Sisters

	Name	Date of birth	Page
1			
2			
3			
4			
5			
6			
7			
8			
9			
10			
11			
12			

Biography

Here you can write a description of the person's life. For example, you can describe the person's education, work, life events, personality, and the places he/she lived.

58. Full name: Genealogical table number:

Surname	
First name	
Gender	
Date of birth	
Place of birth	
Christened	
Occupation	
Date of death	
Place of death	
Date of burial	
Place of burial	

Parents

	Name	Page
Father		
Mother		

Marriage

Name	Place of marriage	Date	Page

Marriages ending in widowhood or divorce

Name	Widowhood or divorce	Date	Page

Children

	Name	Name of co-parent	Page
1			
2			
3			
4			
5			
6			
7			
8			
9			
10			
11			
12			

Brothers & Sisters

	Name	Date of birth	Page
1			
2			
3			
4			
5			
6			
7			
8			
9			
10			
11			
12			

Biography

Here you can write a description of the person's life. For example, you can describe the person's education, work, life events, personality, and the places he/she lived.

59. Full name: **Genealogical table number:**

Surname	
First name	
Gender	
Date of birth	
Place of birth	
Christened	
Occupation	
Date of death	
Place of death	
Date of burial	
Place of burial	

Parents

	Name	Page
Father		
Mother		

Marriage

Name	Place of marriage	Date	Page

Marriages ending in widowhood or divorce

Name	Widowhood or divorce	Date	Page

Children

	Name	Name of co-parent	Page
1			
2			
3			
4			
5			
6			
7			
8			
9			
10			
11			
12			

Brothers & Sisters

	Name	Date of birth	Page
1			
2			
3			
4			
5			
6			
7			
8			
9			
10			
11			
12			

Biography

Here you can write a description of the person's life. For example, you can describe the person's education, work, life events, personality, and the places he/she lived.

60. Full name: **Genealogical table number:**

Surname	
First name	
Gender	
Date of birth	
Place of birth	
Christened	
Occupation	
Date of death	
Place of death	
Date of burial	
Place of burial	

Parents

	Name	Page
Father		
Mother		

Marriage

Name	Place of marriage	Date	Page

Marriages ending in widowhood or divorce

Name	Widowhood or divorce	Date	Page

Children

	Name	Name of co-parent	Page
1			
2			
3			
4			
5			
6			
7			
8			
9			
10			
11			
12			

Brothers & Sisters

	Name	Date of birth	Page
1			
2			
3			
4			
5			
6			
7			
8			
9			
10			
11			
12			

Biography

Here you can write a description of the person's life. For example, you can describe the person's education, work, life events, personality, and the places he/she lived.

61. Full name: Genealogical table number:

Surname	
First name	
Gender	
Date of birth	
Place of birth	
Christened	
Occupation	
Date of death	
Place of death	
Date of burial	
Place of burial	

Parents

	Name	Page
Father		
Mother		

Marriage

Name	Place of marriage	Date	Page

Marriages ending in widowhood or divorce

Name	Widowhood or divorce	Date	Page

Children

	Name	Name of co-parent	Page
1			
2			
3			
4			
5			
6			
7			
8			
9			
10			
11			
12			

Brothers & Sisters

	Name	Date of birth	Page
1			
2			
3			
4			
5			
6			
7			
8			
9			
10			
11			
12			

Biography

Here you can write a description of the person's life. For example, you can describe the person's education, work, life events, personality, and the places he/she lived.

62. Full name: **Genealogical table number:**

Surname	
First name	
Gender	
Date of birth	
Place of birth	
Christened	
Occupation	
Date of death	
Place of death	
Date of burial	
Place of burial	

Parents

	Name	Page
Father		
Mother		

Marriage

Name	Place of marriage	Date	Page

Marriages ending in widowhood or divorce

Name	Widowhood or divorce	Date	Page

Children

	Name	Name of co-parent	Page
1			
2			
3			
4			
5			
6			
7			
8			
9			
10			
11			
12			

Brothers & Sisters

	Name	Date of birth	Page
1			
2			
3			
4			
5			
6			
7			
8			
9			
10			
11			
12			

Biography

Here you can write a description of the person's life. For example, you can describe the person's education, work, life events, personality, and the places he/she lived.

63. Full name: **Genealogical table number:**

Surname	
First name	
Gender	
Date of birth	
Place of birth	
Christened	
Occupation	
Date of death	
Place of death	
Date of burial	
Place of burial	

Parents

	Name	Page
Father		
Mother		

Marriage

Name	Place of marriage	Date	Page

Marriages ending in widowhood or divorce

Name	Widowhood or divorce	Date	Page

Children

	Name	Name of co-parent	Page
1			
2			
3			
4			
5			
6			
7			
8			
9			
10			
11			
12			

Brothers & Sisters

	Name	Date of birth	Page
1			
2			
3			
4			
5			
6			
7			
8			
9			
10			
11			
12			

Biography

Here you can write a description of the person's life. For example, you can describe the person's education, work, life events, personality, and the places he/she lived.

64. Full name: **Genealogical table number:**

Surname	
First name	
Gender	
Date of birth	
Place of birth	
Christened	
Occupation	
Date of death	
Place of death	
Date of burial	
Place of burial	

Parents

	Name	Page
Father		
Mother		

Marriage

Name	Place of marriage	Date	Page

Marriages ending in widowhood or divorce

Name	Widowhood or divorce	Date	Page

Children

	Name	Name of co-parent	Page
1			
2			
3			
4			
5			
6			
7			
8			
9			
10			
11			
12			

Brothers & Sisters

	Name	Date of birth	Page
1			
2			
3			
4			
5			
6			
7			
8			
9			
10			
11			
12			

Biography

Here you can write a description of the person's life. For example, you can describe the person's education, work, life events, personality, and the places he/she lived.

65. Full name: Genealogical table number:

Surname	
First name	
Gender	
Date of birth	
Place of birth	
Christened	
Occupation	
Date of death	
Place of death	
Date of burial	
Place of burial	

Parents

	Name	Page
Father		
Mother		

Marriage

Name	Place of marriage	Date	Page

Marriages ending in widowhood or divorce

Name	Widowhood or divorce	Date	Page

Children

	Name	Name of co-parent	Page
1			
2			
3			
4			
5			
6			
7			
8			
9			
10			
11			
12			

Brothers & Sisters

	Name	Date of birth	Page
1			
2			
3			
4			
5			
6			
7			
8			
9			
10			
11			
12			

Biography

Here you can write a description of the person's life. For example, you can describe the person's education, work, life events, personality, and the places he/she lived.

66. Full name: **Genealogical table number:**

Surname	
First name	
Gender	
Date of birth	
Place of birth	
Christened	
Occupation	
Date of death	
Place of death	
Date of burial	
Place of burial	

Parents

	Name	Page
Father		
Mother		

Marriage

Name	Place of marriage	Date	Page

Marriages ending in widowhood or divorce

Name	Widowhood or divorce	Date	Page

Children

	Name	Name of co-parent	Page
1			
2			
3			
4			
5			
6			
7			
8			
9			
10			
11			
12			

Brothers & Sisters

	Name	Date of birth	Page
1			
2			
3			
4			
5			
6			
7			
8			
9			
10			
11			
12			

Biography

Here you can write a description of the person's life. For example, you can describe the person's education, work, life events, personality, and the places he/she lived.

67. Full name: **Genealogical table number:**

Surname	
First name	
Gender	
Date of birth	
Place of birth	
Christened	
Occupation	
Date of death	
Place of death	
Date of burial	
Place of burial	

Parents

	Name	Page
Father		
Mother		

Marriage

Name	Place of marriage	Date	Page

Marriages ending in widowhood or divorce

Name	Widowhood or divorce	Date	Page

Children

	Name	Name of co-parent	Page
1			
2			
3			
4			
5			
6			
7			
8			
9			
10			
11			
12			

Brothers & Sisters

	Name	Date of birth	Page
1			
2			
3			
4			
5			
6			
7			
8			
9			
10			
11			
12			

Biography

Here you can write a description of the person's life. For example, you can describe the person's education, work, life events, personality, and the places he/she lived.

68. Full name: **Genealogical table number:**

Surname	
First name	
Gender	
Date of birth	
Place of birth	
Christened	
Occupation	
Date of death	
Place of death	
Date of burial	
Place of burial	

Parents

	Name	Page
Father		
Mother		

Marriage

Name	Place of marriage	Date	Page

Marriages ending in widowhood or divorce

Name	Widowhood or divorce	Date	Page

Children

	Name	Name of co-parent	Page
1			
2			
3			
4			
5			
6			
7			
8			
9			
10			
11			
12			

Brothers & Sisters

	Name	Date of birth	Page
1			
2			
3			
4			
5			
6			
7			
8			
9			
10			
11			
12			

Biography

Here you can write a description of the person's life. For example, you can describe the person's education, work, life events, personality, and the places he/she lived.

69. Full name: Genealogical table number:

Surname	
First name	
Gender	
Date of birth	
Place of birth	
Christened	
Occupation	
Date of death	
Place of death	
Date of burial	
Place of burial	

Parents

	Name	Page
Father		
Mother		

Marriage

Name	Place of marriage	Date	Page

Marriages ending in widowhood or divorce

Name	Widowhood or divorce	Date	Page

Children

	Name	Name of co-parent	Page
1			
2			
3			
4			
5			
6			
7			
8			
9			
10			
11			
12			

Brothers & Sisters

	Name	Date of birth	Page
1			
2			
3			
4			
5			
6			
7			
8			
9			
10			
11			
12			

Biography

Here you can write a description of the person's life. For example, you can describe the person's education, work, life events, personality, and the places he/she lived.

70. Full name: **Genealogical table number:**

Surname	
First name	
Gender	
Date of birth	
Place of birth	
Christened	
Occupation	
Date of death	
Place of death	
Date of burial	
Place of burial	

Parents

	Name	Page
Father		
Mother		

Marriage

Name	Place of marriage	Date	Page

Marriages ending in widowhood or divorce

Name	Widowhood or divorce	Date	Page

Children

	Name	Name of co-parent	Page
1			
2			
3			
4			
5			
6			
7			
8			
9			
10			
11			
12			

Brothers & Sisters

	Name	Date of birth	Page
1			
2			
3			
4			
5			
6			
7			
8			
9			
10			
11			
12			

Biography

Here you can write a description of the person's life. For example, you can describe the person's education, work, life events, personality, and the places he/she lived.

71. Full name: **Genealogical table number:**

Surname	
First name	
Gender	
Date of birth	
Place of birth	
Christened	
Occupation	
Date of death	
Place of death	
Date of burial	
Place of burial	

Parents

	Name	Page
Father		
Mother		

Marriage

Name	Place of marriage	Date	Page

Marriages ending in widowhood or divorce

Name	Widowhood or divorce	Date	Page

Children

	Name	Name of co-parent	Page
1			
2			
3			
4			
5			
6			
7			
8			
9			
10			
11			
12			

Brothers & Sisters

	Name	Date of birth	Page
1			
2			
3			
4			
5			
6			
7			
8			
9			
10			
11			
12			

Biography

Here you can write a description of the person's life. For example, you can describe the person's education, work, life events, personality, and the places he/she lived.

72. Full name: **Genealogical table number:**

Surname	
First name	
Gender	
Date of birth	
Place of birth	
Christened	
Occupation	
Date of death	
Place of death	
Date of burial	
Place of burial	

Parents

	Name	Page
Father		
Mother		

Marriage

Name	Place of marriage	Date	Page

Marriages ending in widowhood or divorce

Name	Widowhood or divorce	Date	Page

Children

	Name	Name of co-parent	Page
1			
2			
3			
4			
5			
6			
7			
8			
9			
10			
11			
12			

Brothers & Sisters

	Name	Date of birth	Page
1			
2			
3			
4			
5			
6			
7			
8			
9			
10			
11			
12			

Biography

Here you can write a description of the person's life. For example, you can describe the person's education, work, life events, personality, and the places he/she lived.

73. Full name: Genealogical table number:

Surname	
First name	
Gender	
Date of birth	
Place of birth	
Christened	
Occupation	
Date of death	
Place of death	
Date of burial	
Place of burial	

Parents

	Name	Page
Father		
Mother		

Marriage

Name	Place of marriage	Date	Page

Marriages ending in widowhood or divorce

Name	Widowhood or divorce	Date	Page

Children

	Name	Name of co-parent	Page
1			
2			
3			
4			
5			
6			
7			
8			
9			
10			
11			
12			

Brothers & Sisters

	Name	Date of birth	Page
1			
2			
3			
4			
5			
6			
7			
8			
9			
10			
11			
12			

Biography

Here you can write a description of the person's life. For example, you can describe the person's education, work, life events, personality, and the places he/she lived.

74. Full name: Genealogical table number:

Surname	
First name	
Gender	
Date of birth	
Place of birth	
Christened	
Occupation	
Date of death	
Place of death	
Date of burial	
Place of burial	

Parents

	Name	Page
Father		
Mother		

Marriage

Name	Place of marriage	Date	Page

Marriages ending in widowhood or divorce

Name	Widowhood or divorce	Date	Page

Children

	Name	Name of co-parent	Page
1			
2			
3			
4			
5			
6			
7			
8			
9			
10			
11			
12			

Brothers & Sisters

	Name	Date of birth	Page
1			
2			
3			
4			
5			
6			
7			
8			
9			
10			
11			
12			

Biography

Here you can write a description of the person's life. For example, you can describe the person's education, work, life events, personality, and the places he/she lived.

75. Full name: **Genealogical table number:**

Surname	
First name	
Gender	
Date of birth	
Place of birth	
Christened	
Occupation	
Date of death	
Place of death	
Date of burial	
Place of burial	

Parents

	Name	Page
Father		
Mother		

Marriage

Name	Place of marriage	Date	Page

Marriages ending in widowhood or divorce

Name	Widowhood or divorce	Date	Page

Children

	Name	Name of co-parent	Page
1			
2			
3			
4			
5			
6			
7			
8			
9			
10			
11			
12			

Brothers & Sisters

	Name	Date of birth	Page
1			
2			
3			
4			
5			
6			
7			
8			
9			
10			
11			
12			

Biography

Here you can write a description of the person's life. For example, you can describe the person's education, work, life events, personality, and the places he/she lived.

76. Full name: Genealogical table number:

Surname	
First name	
Gender	
Date of birth	
Place of birth	
Christened	
Occupation	
Date of death	
Place of death	
Date of burial	
Place of burial	

Parents

	Name	Page
Father		
Mother		

Marriage

Name	Place of marriage	Date	Page

Marriages ending in widowhood or divorce

Name	Widowhood or divorce	Date	Page

Children

	Name	Name of co-parent	Page
1			
2			
3			
4			
5			
6			
7			
8			
9			
10			
11			
12			

Brothers & Sisters

	Name	Date of birth	Page
1			
2			
3			
4			
5			
6			
7			
8			
9			
10			
11			
12			

Biography

Here you can write a description of the person's life. For example, you can describe the person's education, work, life events, personality, and the places he/she lived.

77. Full name: **Genealogical table number:**

Surname	
First name	
Gender	
Date of birth	
Place of birth	
Christened	
Occupation	
Date of death	
Place of death	
Date of burial	
Place of burial	

Parents

	Name	Page
Father		
Mother		

Marriage

Name	Place of marriage	Date	Page

Marriages ending in widowhood or divorce

Name	Widowhood or divorce	Date	Page

Children

	Name	Name of co-parent	Page
1			
2			
3			
4			
5			
6			
7			
8			
9			
10			
11			
12			

Brothers & Sisters

	Name	Date of birth	Page
1			
2			
3			
4			
5			
6			
7			
8			
9			
10			
11			
12			

Biography

Here you can write a description of the person's life. For example, you can describe the person's education, work, life events, personality, and the places he/she lived.

78. Full name: Genealogical table number:

Surname	
First name	
Gender	
Date of birth	
Place of birth	
Christened	
Occupation	
Date of death	
Place of death	
Date of burial	
Place of burial	

Parents

	Name	Page
Father		
Mother		

Marriage

Name	Place of marriage	Date	Page

Marriages ending in widowhood or divorce

Name	Widowhood or divorce	Date	Page

Children

	Name	Name of co-parent	Page
1			
2			
3			
4			
5			
6			
7			
8			
9			
10			
11			
12			

Brothers & Sisters

	Name	Date of birth	Page
1			
2			
3			
4			
5			
6			
7			
8			
9			
10			
11			
12			

Biography

Here you can write a description of the person's life. For example, you can describe the person's education, work, life events, personality, and the places he/she lived.

79. Full name: Genealogical table number:

Surname	
First name	
Gender	
Date of birth	
Place of birth	
Christened	
Occupation	
Date of death	
Place of death	
Date of burial	
Place of burial	

Parents

	Name	Page
Father		
Mother		

Marriage

Name	Place of marriage	Date	Page

Marriages ending in widowhood or divorce

Name	Widowhood or divorce	Date	Page

Children

	Name	Name of co-parent	Page
1			
2			
3			
4			
5			
6			
7			
8			
9			
10			
11			
12			

Brothers & Sisters

	Name	Date of birth	Page
1			
2			
3			
4			
5			
6			
7			
8			
9			
10			
11			
12			

Biography

Here you can write a description of the person's life. For example, you can describe the person's education, work, life events, personality, and the places he/she lived.

80. Full name: Genealogical table number:

Surname	
First name	
Gender	
Date of birth	
Place of birth	
Christened	
Occupation	
Date of death	
Place of death	
Date of burial	
Place of burial	

Parents

	Name	Page
Father		
Mother		

Marriage

Name	Place of marriage	Date	Page

Marriages ending in widowhood or divorce

Name	Widowhood or divorce	Date	Page

Children

	Name	Name of co-parent	Page
1			
2			
3			
4			
5			
6			
7			
8			
9			
10			
11			
12			

Brothers & Sisters

	Name	Date of birth	Page
1			
2			
3			
4			
5			
6			
7			
8			
9			
10			
11			
12			

Biography

Here you can write a description of the person's life. For example, you can describe the person's education, work, life events, personality, and the places he/she lived.

81. Full name: Genealogical table number:

Surname	
First name	
Gender	
Date of birth	
Place of birth	
Christened	
Occupation	
Date of death	
Place of death	
Date of burial	
Place of burial	

Parents

	Name	Page
Father		
Mother		

Marriage

Name	Place of marriage	Date	Page

Marriages ending in widowhood or divorce

Name	Widowhood or divorce	Date	Page

Children

	Name	Name of co-parent	Page
1			
2			
3			
4			
5			
6			
7			
8			
9			
10			
11			
12			

Brothers & Sisters

	Name	Date of birth	Page
1			
2			
3			
4			
5			
6			
7			
8			
9			
10			
11			
12			

Biography

Here you can write a description of the person's life. For example, you can describe the person's education, work, life events, personality, and the places he/she lived.

82. Full name: Genealogical table number:

Surname	
First name	
Gender	
Date of birth	
Place of birth	
Christened	
Occupation	
Date of death	
Place of death	
Date of burial	
Place of burial	

Parents

	Name	Page
Father		
Mother		

Marriage

Name	Place of marriage	Date	Page

Marriages ending in widowhood or divorce

Name	Widowhood or divorce	Date	Page

Children

	Name	Name of co-parent	Page
1			
2			
3			
4			
5			
6			
7			
8			
9			
10			
11			
12			

Brothers & Sisters

	Name	Date of birth	Page
1			
2			
3			
4			
5			
6			
7			
8			
9			
10			
11			
12			

Biography

Here you can write a description of the person's life. For example, you can describe the person's education, work, life events, personality, and the places he/she lived.

83. Full name: Genealogical table number:

Surname	
First name	
Gender	
Date of birth	
Place of birth	
Christened	
Occupation	
Date of death	
Place of death	
Date of burial	
Place of burial	

Parents

	Name	Page
Father		
Mother		

Marriage

Name	Place of marriage	Date	Page

Marriages ending in widowhood or divorce

Name	Widowhood or divorce	Date	Page

Children

	Name	Name of co-parent	Page
1			
2			
3			
4			
5			
6			
7			
8			
9			
10			
11			
12			

Brothers & Sisters

	Name	Date of birth	Page
1			
2			
3			
4			
5			
6			
7			
8			
9			
10			
11			
12			

Biography

Here you can write a description of the person's life. For example, you can describe the person's education, work, life events, personality, and the places he/she lived.

84. Full name: **Genealogical table number:**

Surname	
First name	
Gender	
Date of birth	
Place of birth	
Christened	
Occupation	
Date of death	
Place of death	
Date of burial	
Place of burial	

Parents

	Name	Page
Father		
Mother		

Marriage

Name	Place of marriage	Date	Page

Marriages ending in widowhood or divorce

Name	Widowhood or divorce	Date	Page

Children

	Name	Name of co-parent	Page
1			
2			
3			
4			
5			
6			
7			
8			
9			
10			
11			
12			

Brothers & Sisters

	Name	Date of birth	Page
1			
2			
3			
4			
5			
6			
7			
8			
9			
10			
11			
12			

Biography

Here you can write a description of the person's life. For example, you can describe the person's education, work, life events, personality, and the places he/she lived.

85. Full name: Genealogical table number:

Surname	
First name	
Gender	
Date of birth	
Place of birth	
Christened	
Occupation	
Date of death	
Place of death	
Date of burial	
Place of burial	

Parents

	Name	Page
Father		
Mother		

Marriage

Name	Place of marriage	Date	Page

Marriages ending in widowhood or divorce

Name	Widowhood or divorce	Date	Page

Children

	Name	Name of co-parent	Page
1			
2			
3			
4			
5			
6			
7			
8			
9			
10			
11			
12			

Brothers & Sisters

	Name	Date of birth	Page
1			
2			
3			
4			
5			
6			
7			
8			
9			
10			
11			
12			

Biography

Here you can write a description of the person's life. For example, you can describe the person's education, work, life events, personality, and the places he/she lived.

86. Full name: Genealogical table number:

Surname	
First name	
Gender	
Date of birth	
Place of birth	
Christened	
Occupation	
Date of death	
Place of death	
Date of burial	
Place of burial	

Parents

	Name	Page
Father		
Mother		

Marriage

Name	Place of marriage	Date	Page

Marriages ending in widowhood or divorce

Name	Widowhood or divorce	Date	Page

Children

	Name	Name of co-parent	Page
1			
2			
3			
4			
5			
6			
7			
8			
9			
10			
11			
12			

Brothers & Sisters

	Name	Date of birth	Page
1			
2			
3			
4			
5			
6			
7			
8			
9			
10			
11			
12			

Biography

Here you can write a description of the person's life. For example, you can describe the person's education, work, life events, personality, and the places he/she lived.

87. Full name: Genealogical table number:

Surname	
First name	
Gender	
Date of birth	
Place of birth	
Christened	
Occupation	
Date of death	
Place of death	
Date of burial	
Place of burial	

Parents

	Name	Page
Father		
Mother		

Marriage

Name	Place of marriage	Date	Page

Marriages ending in widowhood or divorce

Name	Widowhood or divorce	Date	Page

Children

	Name	Name of co-parent	Page
1			
2			
3			
4			
5			
6			
7			
8			
9			
10			
11			
12			

Brothers & Sisters

	Name	Date of birth	Page
1			
2			
3			
4			
5			
6			
7			
8			
9			
10			
11			
12			

Biography

Here you can write a description of the person's life. For example, you can describe the person's education, work, life events, personality, and the places he/she lived.

88. Full name: Genealogical table number:

Surname	
First name	
Gender	
Date of birth	
Place of birth	
Christened	
Occupation	
Date of death	
Place of death	
Date of burial	
Place of burial	

Parents

	Name	Page
Father		
Mother		

Marriage

Name	Place of marriage	Date	Page

Marriages ending in widowhood or divorce

Name	Widowhood or divorce	Date	Page

Children

	Name	Name of co-parent	Page
1			
2			
3			
4			
5			
6			
7			
8			
9			
10			
11			
12			

Brothers & Sisters

	Name	Date of birth	Page
1			
2			
3			
4			
5			
6			
7			
8			
9			
10			
11			
12			

Biography

Here you can write a description of the person's life. For example, you can describe the person's education, work, life events, personality, and the places he/she lived.

89. Full name: **Genealogical table number:**

Surname	
First name	
Gender	
Date of birth	
Place of birth	
Christened	
Occupation	
Date of death	
Place of death	
Date of burial	
Place of burial	

Parents

	Name	Page
Father		
Mother		

Marriage

Name	Place of marriage	Date	Page

Marriages ending in widowhood or divorce

Name	Widowhood or divorce	Date	Page

Children

	Name	Name of co-parent	Page
1			
2			
3			
4			
5			
6			
7			
8			
9			
10			
11			
12			

Brothers & Sisters

	Name	Date of birth	Page
1			
2			
3			
4			
5			
6			
7			
8			
9			
10			
11			
12			

Biography

Here you can write a description of the person's life. For example, you can describe the person's education, work, life events, personality, and the places he/she lived.

90. Full name: **Genealogical table number:**

Surname	
First name	
Gender	
Date of birth	
Place of birth	
Christened	
Occupation	
Date of death	
Place of death	
Date of burial	
Place of burial	

Parents

	Name	Page
Father		
Mother		

Marriage

Name	Place of marriage	Date	Page

Marriages ending in widowhood or divorce

Name	Widowhood or divorce	Date	Page

Children

	Name	Name of co-parent	Page
1			
2			
3			
4			
5			
6			
7			
8			
9			
10			
11			
12			

Brothers & Sisters

	Name	Date of birth	Page
1			
2			
3			
4			
5			
6			
7			
8			
9			
10			
11			
12			

Biography
Here you can write a description of the person's life. For example, you can describe the person's education, work, life events, personality, and the places he/she lived.

91. Full name: Genealogical table number:

Surname	
First name	
Gender	
Date of birth	
Place of birth	
Christened	
Occupation	
Date of death	
Place of death	
Date of burial	
Place of burial	

Parents

	Name	Page
Father		
Mother		

Marriage

Name	Place of marriage	Date	Page

Marriages ending in widowhood or divorce

Name	Widowhood or divorce	Date	Page

Children

	Name	Name of co-parent	Page
1			
2			
3			
4			
5			
6			
7			
8			
9			
10			
11			
12			

Brothers & Sisters

	Name	Date of birth	Page
1			
2			
3			
4			
5			
6			
7			
8			
9			
10			
11			
12			

Biography

Here you can write a description of the person's life. For example, you can describe the person's education, work, life events, personality, and the places he/she lived.

92. Full name: **Genealogical table number:**

Surname	
First name	
Gender	
Date of birth	
Place of birth	
Christened	
Occupation	
Date of death	
Place of death	
Date of burial	
Place of burial	

Parents

	Name	Page
Father		
Mother		

Marriage

Name	Place of marriage	Date	Page

Marriages ending in widowhood or divorce

Name	Widowhood or divorce	Date	Page

Children

	Name	Name of co-parent	Page
1			
2			
3			
4			
5			
6			
7			
8			
9			
10			
11			
12			

Brothers & Sisters

	Name	Date of birth	Page
1			
2			
3			
4			
5			
6			
7			
8			
9			
10			
11			
12			

Biography

Here you can write a description of the person's life. For example, you can describe the person's education, work, life events, personality, and the places he/she lived.

93. Full name:　　　　　　　　　　　　　　　　**Genealogical table number:**

Surname	
First name	
Gender	
Date of birth	
Place of birth	
Christened	
Occupation	
Date of death	
Place of death	
Date of burial	
Place of burial	

Parents

	Name	Page
Father		
Mother		

Marriage

Name	Place of marriage	Date	Page

Marriages ending in widowhood or divorce

Name	Widowhood or divorce	Date	Page

Children

	Name	Name of co-parent	Page
1			
2			
3			
4			
5			
6			
7			
8			
9			
10			
11			
12			

Brothers & Sisters

	Name	Date of birth	Page
1			
2			
3			
4			
5			
6			
7			
8			
9			
10			
11			
12			

Biography

Here you can write a description of the person's life. For example, you can describe the person's education, work, life events, personality, and the places he/she lived.

94. Full name: **Genealogical table number:**

Surname	
First name	
Gender	
Date of birth	
Place of birth	
Christened	
Occupation	
Date of death	
Place of death	
Date of burial	
Place of burial	

Parents

	Name	Page
Father		
Mother		

Marriage

Name	Place of marriage	Date	Page

Marriages ending in widowhood or divorce

Name	Widowhood or divorce	Date	Page

Children

	Name	Name of co-parent	Page
1			
2			
3			
4			
5			
6			
7			
8			
9			
10			
11			
12			

Brothers & Sisters

	Name	Date of birth	Page
1			
2			
3			
4			
5			
6			
7			
8			
9			
10			
11			
12			

Biography

Here you can write a description of the person's life. For example, you can describe the person's education, work, life events, personality, and the places he/she lived.

95. Full name: **Genealogical table number:**

Surname	
First name	
Gender	
Date of birth	
Place of birth	
Christened	
Occupation	
Date of death	
Place of death	
Date of burial	
Place of burial	

Parents

	Name	Page
Father		
Mother		

Marriage

Name	Place of marriage	Date	Page

Marriages ending in widowhood or divorce

Name	Widowhood or divorce	Date	Page

Children

	Name	Name of co-parent	Page
1			
2			
3			
4			
5			
6			
7			
8			
9			
10			
11			
12			

Brothers & Sisters

	Name	Date of birth	Page
1			
2			
3			
4			
5			
6			
7			
8			
9			
10			
11			
12			

Biography

Here you can write a description of the person's life. For example, you can describe the person's education, work, life events, personality, and the places he/she lived.

96. Full name: **Genealogical table number:**

Surname	
First name	
Gender	
Date of birth	
Place of birth	
Christened	
Occupation	
Date of death	
Place of death	
Date of burial	
Place of burial	

Parents

	Name	Page
Father		
Mother		

Marriage

Name	Place of marriage	Date	Page

Marriages ending in widowhood or divorce

Name	Widowhood or divorce	Date	Page

Children

	Name	Name of co-parent	Page
1			
2			
3			
4			
5			
6			
7			
8			
9			
10			
11			
12			

Brothers & Sisters

	Name	Date of birth	Page
1			
2			
3			
4			
5			
6			
7			
8			
9			
10			
11			
12			

Biography

Here you can write a description of the person's life. For example, you can describe the person's education, work, life events, personality, and the places he/she lived.

97. Full name: **Genealogical table number:**

Surname	
First name	
Gender	
Date of birth	
Place of birth	
Christened	
Occupation	
Date of death	
Place of death	
Date of burial	
Place of burial	

Parents

	Name	Page
Father		
Mother		

Marriage

Name	Place of marriage	Date	Page

Marriages ending in widowhood or divorce

Name	Widowhood or divorce	Date	Page

Children

	Name	Name of co-parent	Page
1			
2			
3			
4			
5			
6			
7			
8			
9			
10			
11			
12			

Brothers & Sisters

	Name	Date of birth	Page
1			
2			
3			
4			
5			
6			
7			
8			
9			
10			
11			
12			

Biography

Here you can write a description of the person's life. For example, you can describe the person's education, work, life events, personality, and the places he/she lived.

98. Full name: **Genealogical table number:**

Surname	
First name	
Gender	
Date of birth	
Place of birth	
Christened	
Occupation	
Date of death	
Place of death	
Date of burial	
Place of burial	

Parents

	Name	Page
Father		
Mother		

Marriage

Name	Place of marriage	Date	Page

Marriages ending in widowhood or divorce

Name	Widowhood or divorce	Date	Page

Children

	Name	Name of co-parent	Page
1			
2			
3			
4			
5			
6			
7			
8			
9			
10			
11			
12			

Brothers & Sisters

	Name	Date of birth	Page
1			
2			
3			
4			
5			
6			
7			
8			
9			
10			
11			
12			

Biography

Here you can write a description of the person's life. For example, you can describe the person's education, work, life events, personality, and the places he/she lived.

99. Full name: **Genealogical table number:**

Surname	
First name	
Gender	
Date of birth	
Place of birth	
Christened	
Occupation	
Date of death	
Place of death	
Date of burial	
Place of burial	

Parents

	Name	Page
Father		
Mother		

Marriage

Name	Place of marriage	Date	Page

Marriages ending in widowhood or divorce

Name	Widowhood or divorce	Date	Page

Children

	Name	Name of co-parent	Page
1			
2			
3			
4			
5			
6			
7			
8			
9			
10			
11			
12			

Brothers & Sisters

	Name	Date of birth	Page
1			
2			
3			
4			
5			
6			
7			
8			
9			
10			
11			
12			

Biography

Here you can write a description of the person's life. For example, you can describe the person's education, work, life events, personality, and the places he/she lived.

100.   Full name: Genealogical table number:

Surname	
First name	
Gender	
Date of birth	
Place of birth	
Christened	
Occupation	
Date of death	
Place of death	
Date of burial	
Place of burial	

Parents

	Name	Page
Father		
Mother		

Marriage

Name	Place of marriage	Date	Page

Marriages ending in widowhood or divorce

Name	Widowhood or divorce	Date	Page

Children

	Name	Name of co-parent	Page
1			
2			
3			
4			
5			
6			
7			
8			
9			
10			
11			
12			

Brothers & Sisters

	Name	Date of birth	Page
1			
2			
3			
4			
5			
6			
7			
8			
9			
10			
11			
12			

Biography

Here you can write a description of the person's life. For example, you can describe the person's education, work, life events, personality, and the places he/she lived.

101. Full name: Genealogical table number:

Surname	
First name	
Gender	
Date of birth	
Place of birth	
Christened	
Occupation	
Date of death	
Place of death	
Date of burial	
Place of burial	

Parents

	Name	Page
Father		
Mother		

Marriage

Name	Place of marriage	Date	Page

Marriages ending in widowhood or divorce

Name	Widowhood or divorce	Date	Page

Children

	Name	Name of co-parent	Page
1			
2			
3			
4			
5			
6			
7			
8			
9			
10			
11			
12			

Brothers & Sisters

	Name	Date of birth	Page
1			
2			
3			
4			
5			
6			
7			
8			
9			
10			
11			
12			

Biography

Here you can write a description of the person's life. For example, you can describe the person's education, work, life events, personality, and the places he/she lived.

102.   Full name: Genealogical table number:

Surname	
First name	
Gender	
Date of birth	
Place of birth	
Christened	
Occupation	
Date of death	
Place of death	
Date of burial	
Place of burial	

Parents

	Name	Page
Father		
Mother		

Marriage

Name	Place of marriage	Date	Page

Marriages ending in widowhood or divorce

Name	Widowhood or divorce	Date	Page

Children

	Name	Name of co-parent	Page
1			
2			
3			
4			
5			
6			
7			
8			
9			
10			
11			
12			

Brothers & Sisters

	Name	Date of birth	Page
1			
2			
3			
4			
5			
6			
7			
8			
9			
10			
11			
12			

Biography

Here you can write a description of the person's life. For example, you can describe the person's education, work, life events, personality, and the places he/she lived.

103. Full name: Genealogical table number:

Surname	
First name	
Gender	
Date of birth	
Place of birth	
Christened	
Occupation	
Date of death	
Place of death	
Date of burial	
Place of burial	

Parents

	Name	Page
Father		
Mother		

Marriage

Name	Place of marriage	Date	Page

Marriages ending in widowhood or divorce

Name	Widowhood or divorce	Date	Page

Children

	Name	Name of co-parent	Page
1			
2			
3			
4			
5			
6			
7			
8			
9			
10			
11			
12			

Brothers & Sisters

	Name	Date of birth	Page
1			
2			
3			
4			
5			
6			
7			
8			
9			
10			
11			
12			

Biography

Here you can write a description of the person's life. For example, you can describe the person's education, work, life events, personality, and the places he/she lived.

104.　　　Full name:　　　　　　　　　　　　Genealogical table number:

Surname	
First name	
Gender	
Date of birth	
Place of birth	
Christened	
Occupation	
Date of death	
Place of death	
Date of burial	
Place of burial	

Parents

	Name	Page
Father		
Mother		

Marriage

Name	Place of marriage	Date	Page

Marriages ending in widowhood or divorce

Name	Widowhood or divorce	Date	Page

Children

	Name	Name of co-parent	Page
1			
2			
3			
4			
5			
6			
7			
8			
9			
10			
11			
12			

Brothers & Sisters

	Name	Date of birth	Page
1			
2			
3			
4			
5			
6			
7			
8			
9			
10			
11			
12			

Biography

Here you can write a description of the person's life. For example, you can describe the person's education, work, life events, personality, and the places he/she lived.

105. Full name: Genealogical table number:

Surname	
First name	
Gender	
Date of birth	
Place of birth	
Christened	
Occupation	
Date of death	
Place of death	
Date of burial	
Place of burial	

Parents

	Name	Page
Father		
Mother		

Marriage

Name	Place of marriage	Date	Page

Marriages ending in widowhood or divorce

Name	Widowhood or divorce	Date	Page

Children

	Name	Name of co-parent	Page
1			
2			
3			
4			
5			
6			
7			
8			
9			
10			
11			
12			

Brothers & Sisters

	Name	Date of birth	Page
1			
2			
3			
4			
5			
6			
7			
8			
9			
10			
11			
12			

Biography

Here you can write a description of the person's life. For example, you can describe the person's education, work, life events, personality, and the places he/she lived.

106. Full name: Genealogical table number:

Surname	
First name	
Gender	
Date of birth	
Place of birth	
Christened	
Occupation	
Date of death	
Place of death	
Date of burial	
Place of burial	

Parents

	Name	Page
Father		
Mother		

Marriage

Name	Place of marriage	Date	Page

Marriages ending in widowhood or divorce

Name	Widowhood or divorce	Date	Page

Children

	Name	Name of co-parent	Page
1			
2			
3			
4			
5			
6			
7			
8			
9			
10			
11			
12			

Brothers & Sisters

	Name	Date of birth	Page
1			
2			
3			
4			
5			
6			
7			
8			
9			
10			
11			
12			

Biography

Here you can write a description of the person's life. For example, you can describe the person's education, work, life events, personality, and the places he/she lived.

107. Full name: Genealogical table number:

Surname	
First name	
Gender	
Date of birth	
Place of birth	
Christened	
Occupation	
Date of death	
Place of death	
Date of burial	
Place of burial	

Parents

	Name	Page
Father		
Mother		

Marriage

Name	Place of marriage	Date	Page

Marriages ending in widowhood or divorce

Name	Widowhood or divorce	Date	Page

Children

	Name	Name of co-parent	Page
1			
2			
3			
4			
5			
6			
7			
8			
9			
10			
11			
12			

Brothers & Sisters

	Name	Date of birth	Page
1			
2			
3			
4			
5			
6			
7			
8			
9			
10			
11			
12			

Biography

Here you can write a description of the person's life. For example, you can describe the person's education, work, life events, personality, and the places he/she lived.

108. Full name: Genealogical table number:

Surname	
First name	
Gender	
Date of birth	
Place of birth	
Christened	
Occupation	
Date of death	
Place of death	
Date of burial	
Place of burial	

Parents

	Name	Page
Father		
Mother		

Marriage

Name	Place of marriage	Date	Page

Marriages ending in widowhood or divorce

Name	Widowhood or divorce	Date	Page

Children

	Name	Name of co-parent	Page
1			
2			
3			
4			
5			
6			
7			
8			
9			
10			
11			
12			

Brothers & Sisters

	Name	Date of birth	Page
1			
2			
3			
4			
5			
6			
7			
8			
9			
10			
11			
12			

Biography

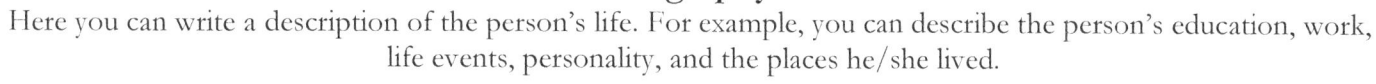

Here you can write a description of the person's life. For example, you can describe the person's education, work, life events, personality, and the places he/she lived.

109. Full name: Genealogical table number:

Surname	
First name	
Gender	
Date of birth	
Place of birth	
Christened	
Occupation	
Date of death	
Place of death	
Date of burial	
Place of burial	

Parents

	Name	Page
Father		
Mother		

Marriage

Name	Place of marriage	Date	Page

Marriages ending in widowhood or divorce

Name	Widowhood or divorce	Date	Page

Children

	Name	Name of co-parent	Page
1			
2			
3			
4			
5			
6			
7			
8			
9			
10			
11			
12			

Brothers & Sisters

	Name	Date of birth	Page
1			
2			
3			
4			
5			
6			
7			
8			
9			
10			
11			
12			

Biography

Here you can write a description of the person's life. For example, you can describe the person's education, work, life events, personality, and the places he/she lived.

110.   Full name: Genealogical table number:

Surname	
First name	
Gender	
Date of birth	
Place of birth	
Christened	
Occupation	
Date of death	
Place of death	
Date of burial	
Place of burial	

Parents

	Name	Page
Father		
Mother		

Marriage

Name	Place of marriage	Date	Page

Marriages ending in widowhood or divorce

Name	Widowhood or divorce	Date	Page

Children

	Name	Name of co-parent	Page
1			
2			
3			
4			
5			
6			
7			
8			
9			
10			
11			
12			

Brothers & Sisters

	Name	Date of birth	Page
1			
2			
3			
4			
5			
6			
7			
8			
9			
10			
11			
12			

Biography

Here you can write a description of the person's life. For example, you can describe the person's education, work, life events, personality, and the places he/she lived.

111. Full name: Genealogical table number:

Surname	
First name	
Gender	
Date of birth	
Place of birth	
Christened	
Occupation	
Date of death	
Place of death	
Date of burial	
Place of burial	

Parents

	Name	Page
Father		
Mother		

Marriage

Name	Place of marriage	Date	Page

Marriages ending in widowhood or divorce

Name	Widowhood or divorce	Date	Page

Children

	Name	Name of co-parent	Page
1			
2			
3			
4			
5			
6			
7			
8			
9			
10			
11			
12			

Brothers & Sisters

	Name	Date of birth	Page
1			
2			
3			
4			
5			
6			
7			
8			
9			
10			
11			
12			

Biography

Here you can write a description of the person's life. For example, you can describe the person's education, work, life events, personality, and the places he/she lived.

112. Full name: Genealogical table number:

Surname	
First name	
Gender	
Date of birth	
Place of birth	
Christened	
Occupation	
Date of death	
Place of death	
Date of burial	
Place of burial	

Parents

	Name	Page
Father		
Mother		

Marriage

Name	Place of marriage	Date	Page

Marriages ending in widowhood or divorce

Name	Widowhood or divorce	Date	Page

Children

	Name	Name of co-parent	Page
1			
2			
3			
4			
5			
6			
7			
8			
9			
10			
11			
12			

Brothers & Sisters

	Name	Date of birth	Page
1			
2			
3			
4			
5			
6			
7			
8			
9			
10			
11			
12			

Biography

Here you can write a description of the person's life. For example, you can describe the person's education, work, life events, personality, and the places he/she lived.

113.   Full name: Genealogical table number:

Surname	
First name	
Gender	
Date of birth	
Place of birth	
Christened	
Occupation	
Date of death	
Place of death	
Date of burial	
Place of burial	

Parents

	Name	Page
Father		
Mother		

Marriage

Name	Place of marriage	Date	Page

Marriages ending in widowhood or divorce

Name	Widowhood or divorce	Date	Page

Children

	Name	Name of co-parent	Page
1			
2			
3			
4			
5			
6			
7			
8			
9			
10			
11			
12			

Brothers & Sisters

	Name	Date of birth	Page
1			
2			
3			
4			
5			
6			
7			
8			
9			
10			
11			
12			

Biography

Here you can write a description of the person's life. For example, you can describe the person's education, work, life events, personality, and the places he/she lived.

114.   Full name: Genealogical table number:

Surname	
First name	
Gender	
Date of birth	
Place of birth	
Christened	
Occupation	
Date of death	
Place of death	
Date of burial	
Place of burial	

Parents

	Name	Page
Father		
Mother		

Marriage

Name	Place of marriage	Date	Page

Marriages ending in widowhood or divorce

Name	Widowhood or divorce	Date	Page

Children

	Name	Name of co-parent	Page
1			
2			
3			
4			
5			
6			
7			
8			
9			
10			
11			
12			

Brothers & Sisters

	Name	Date of birth	Page
1			
2			
3			
4			
5			
6			
7			
8			
9			
10			
11			
12			

Biography

Here you can write a description of the person's life. For example, you can describe the person's education, work, life events, personality, and the places he/she lived.

115. Full name: Genealogical table number:

Surname	
First name	
Gender	
Date of birth	
Place of birth	
Christened	
Occupation	
Date of death	
Place of death	
Date of burial	
Place of burial	

Parents

	Name	Page
Father		
Mother		

Marriage

Name	Place of marriage	Date	Page

Marriages ending in widowhood or divorce

Name	Widowhood or divorce	Date	Page

Children

	Name	Name of co-parent	Page
1			
2			
3			
4			
5			
6			
7			
8			
9			
10			
11			
12			

Brothers & Sisters

	Name	Date of birth	Page
1			
2			
3			
4			
5			
6			
7			
8			
9			
10			
11			
12			

Biography

Here you can write a description of the person's life. For example, you can describe the person's education, work, life events, personality, and the places he/she lived.

116.   Full name: Genealogical table number:

Surname	
First name	
Gender	
Date of birth	
Place of birth	
Christened	
Occupation	
Date of death	
Place of death	
Date of burial	
Place of burial	

Parents

	Name	Page
Father		
Mother		

Marriage

Name	Place of marriage	Date	Page

Marriages ending in widowhood or divorce

Name	Widowhood or divorce	Date	Page

Children

	Name	Name of co-parent	Page
1			
2			
3			
4			
5			
6			
7			
8			
9			
10			
11			
12			

Brothers & Sisters

	Name	Date of birth	Page
1			
2			
3			
4			
5			
6			
7			
8			
9			
10			
11			
12			

Biography

Here you can write a description of the person's life. For example, you can describe the person's education, work, life events, personality, and the places he/she lived.

117. Full name: Genealogical table number:

Surname	
First name	
Gender	
Date of birth	
Place of birth	
Christened	
Occupation	
Date of death	
Place of death	
Date of burial	
Place of burial	

Parents

	Name	Page
Father		
Mother		

Marriage

Name	Place of marriage	Date	Page

Marriages ending in widowhood or divorce

Name	Widowhood or divorce	Date	Page

Children

	Name	Name of co-parent	Page
1			
2			
3			
4			
5			
6			
7			
8			
9			
10			
11			
12			

Brothers & Sisters

	Name	Date of birth	Page
1			
2			
3			
4			
5			
6			
7			
8			
9			
10			
11			
12			

Biography

Here you can write a description of the person's life. For example, you can describe the person's education, work, life events, personality, and the places he/she lived.

118.   Full name: Genealogical table number:

Surname	
First name	
Gender	
Date of birth	
Place of birth	
Christened	
Occupation	
Date of death	
Place of death	
Date of burial	
Place of burial	

Parents

	Name	Page
Father		
Mother		

Marriage

Name	Place of marriage	Date	Page

Marriages ending in widowhood or divorce

Name	Widowhood or divorce	Date	Page

Children

	Name	Name of co-parent	Page
1			
2			
3			
4			
5			
6			
7			
8			
9			
10			
11			
12			

Brothers & Sisters

	Name	Date of birth	Page
1			
2			
3			
4			
5			
6			
7			
8			
9			
10			
11			
12			

Biography

Here you can write a description of the person's life. For example, you can describe the person's education, work, life events, personality, and the places he/she lived.

119.   **Full name:**   **Genealogical table number:**

Surname	
First name	
Gender	
Date of birth	
Place of birth	
Christened	
Occupation	
Date of death	
Place of death	
Date of burial	
Place of burial	

Parents

	Name	Page
Father		
Mother		

Marriage

Name	Place of marriage	Date	Page

Marriages ending in widowhood or divorce

Name	Widowhood or divorce	Date	Page

Children

	Name	Name of co-parent	Page
1			
2			
3			
4			
5			
6			
7			
8			
9			
10			
11			
12			

Brothers & Sisters

	Name	Date of birth	Page
1			
2			
3			
4			
5			
6			
7			
8			
9			
10			
11			
12			

Biography

Here you can write a description of the person's life. For example, you can describe the person's education, work, life events, personality, and the places he/she lived.

120. Full name: Genealogical table number:

Surname	
First name	
Gender	
Date of birth	
Place of birth	
Christened	
Occupation	
Date of death	
Place of death	
Date of burial	
Place of burial	

Parents

	Name	Page
Father		
Mother		

Marriage

Name	Place of marriage	Date	Page

Marriages ending in widowhood or divorce

Name	Widowhood or divorce	Date	Page

Children

	Name	Name of co-parent	Page
1			
2			
3			
4			
5			
6			
7			
8			
9			
10			
11			
12			

Brothers & Sisters

	Name	Date of birth	Page
1			
2			
3			
4			
5			
6			
7			
8			
9			
10			
11			
12			

Biography

Here you can write a description of the person's life. For example, you can describe the person's education, work, life events, personality, and the places he/she lived.

121. Full name: Genealogical table number:

Surname	
First name	
Gender	
Date of birth	
Place of birth	
Christened	
Occupation	
Date of death	
Place of death	
Date of burial	
Place of burial	

Parents

	Name	Page
Father		
Mother		

Marriage

Name	Place of marriage	Date	Page

Marriages ending in widowhood or divorce

Name	Widowhood or divorce	Date	Page

Children

	Name	Name of co-parent	Page
1			
2			
3			
4			
5			
6			
7			
8			
9			
10			
11			
12			

Brothers & Sisters

	Name	Date of birth	Page
1			
2			
3			
4			
5			
6			
7			
8			
9			
10			
11			
12			

Biography

Here you can write a description of the person's life. For example, you can describe the person's education, work, life events, personality, and the places he/she lived.

122. Full name: Genealogical table number:

Surname	
First name	
Gender	
Date of birth	
Place of birth	
Christened	
Occupation	
Date of death	
Place of death	
Date of burial	
Place of burial	

Parents

	Name	Page
Father		
Mother		

Marriage

Name	Place of marriage	Date	Page

Marriages ending in widowhood or divorce

Name	Widowhood or divorce	Date	Page

Children

	Name	Name of co-parent	Page
1			
2			
3			
4			
5			
6			
7			
8			
9			
10			
11			
12			

Brothers & Sisters

	Name	Date of birth	Page
1			
2			
3			
4			
5			
6			
7			
8			
9			
10			
11			
12			

Biography

Here you can write a description of the person's life. For example, you can describe the person's education, work, life events, personality, and the places he/she lived.

123. Full name: Genealogical table number:

Surname	
First name	
Gender	
Date of birth	
Place of birth	
Christened	
Occupation	
Date of death	
Place of death	
Date of burial	
Place of burial	

Parents

	Name	Page
Father		
Mother		

Marriage

Name	Place of marriage	Date	Page

Marriages ending in widowhood or divorce

Name	Widowhood or divorce	Date	Page

Children

	Name	Name of co-parent	Page
1			
2			
3			
4			
5			
6			
7			
8			
9			
10			
11			
12			

Brothers & Sisters

	Name	Date of birth	Page
1			
2			
3			
4			
5			
6			
7			
8			
9			
10			
11			
12			

Biography

Here you can write a description of the person's life. For example, you can describe the person's education, work, life events, personality, and the places he/she lived.

124.   Full name: Genealogical table number:

Surname	
First name	
Gender	
Date of birth	
Place of birth	
Christened	
Occupation	
Date of death	
Place of death	
Date of burial	
Place of burial	

Parents

	Name	Page
Father		
Mother		

Marriage

Name	Place of marriage	Date	Page

Marriages ending in widowhood or divorce

Name	Widowhood or divorce	Date	Page

Children

	Name	Name of co-parent	Page
1			
2			
3			
4			
5			
6			
7			
8			
9			
10			
11			
12			

Brothers & Sisters

	Name	Date of birth	Page
1			
2			
3			
4			
5			
6			
7			
8			
9			
10			
11			
12			

Biography

Here you can write a description of the person's life. For example, you can describe the person's education, work, life events, personality, and the places he/she lived.

125. Full name: Genealogical table number:

Surname	
First name	
Gender	
Date of birth	
Place of birth	
Christened	
Occupation	
Date of death	
Place of death	
Date of burial	
Place of burial	

Parents

	Name	Page
Father		
Mother		

Marriage

Name	Place of marriage	Date	Page

Marriages ending in widowhood or divorce

Name	Widowhood or divorce	Date	Page

Children

	Name	Name of co-parent	Page
1			
2			
3			
4			
5			
6			
7			
8			
9			
10			
11			
12			

Brothers & Sisters

	Name	Date of birth	Page
1			
2			
3			
4			
5			
6			
7			
8			
9			
10			
11			
12			

Biography

Here you can write a description of the person's life. For example, you can describe the person's education, work, life events, personality, and the places he/she lived.

126. Full name: Genealogical table number:

Surname	
First name	
Gender	
Date of birth	
Place of birth	
Christened	
Occupation	
Date of death	
Place of death	
Date of burial	
Place of burial	

Parents

	Name	Page
Father		
Mother		

Marriage

Name	Place of marriage	Date	Page

Marriages ending in widowhood or divorce

Name	Widowhood or divorce	Date	Page

Children

	Name	Name of co-parent	Page
1			
2			
3			
4			
5			
6			
7			
8			
9			
10			
11			
12			

Brothers & Sisters

	Name	Date of birth	Page
1			
2			
3			
4			
5			
6			
7			
8			
9			
10			
11			
12			

Biography
Here you can write a description of the person's life. For example, you can describe the person's education, work, life events, personality, and the places he/she lived.

127. Full name: Genealogical table number:

Surname	
First name	
Gender	
Date of birth	
Place of birth	
Christened	
Occupation	
Date of death	
Place of death	
Date of burial	
Place of burial	

Parents

	Name	Page
Father		
Mother		

Marriage

Name	Place of marriage	Date	Page

Marriages ending in widowhood or divorce

Name	Widowhood or divorce	Date	Page

Children

	Name	Name of co-parent	Page
1			
2			
3			
4			
5			
6			
7			
8			
9			
10			
11			
12			

Brothers & Sisters

	Name	Date of birth	Page
1			
2			
3			
4			
5			
6			
7			
8			
9			
10			
11			
12			

Biography

Here you can write a description of the person's life. For example, you can describe the person's education, work, life events, personality, and the places he/she lived.

Chapter 2: Alternate name spellings

In older records, you'll often find names spelled in a variety of ways, even in the same document. In particular, immigrants' records of entry into the United States often contain assumed or incorrect names.
In this chapter you can record the various spellings of each name.

Name:
Alternate spellings:

1	
2	
3	
4	
5	

Name:
Alternate spellings:

1	
2	
3	
4	
5	

Name:
Alternate spellings:

1	
2	
3	
4	
5	

Name:
Alternate spellings:

1	
2	
3	
4	
5	

Name:
Alternate spellings:

1	
2	
3	
4	
5	

Name:
Alternate spellings:

1	
2	
3	
4	
5	

Name:
Alternate spellings:

1	
2	
3	
4	
5	

Name:
Alternate spellings:

1	
2	
3	
4	
5	

Name:
Alternate spellings:

1	
2	
3	
4	
5	

Name:
Alternate spellings:

1	
2	
3	
4	
5	

Name:
Alternate spellings:

1	
2	
3	
4	
5	

Name:
Alternate spellings:

1	
2	
3	
4	
5	

Name:
Alternate spellings:

1	
2	
3	
4	
5	

Name:
Alternate spellings:

1	
2	
3	
4	
5	

Name:
Alternate spellings:

1	
2	
3	
4	
5	

Name:
Alternate spellings:

1	
2	
3	
4	
5	

Name:
Alternate spellings:

1	
2	
3	
4	
5	

Name:
Alternate spellings:

1	
2	
3	
4	
5	

Name:
Alternate spellings:

1	
2	
3	
4	
5	

Name:
Alternate spellings:

1	
2	
3	
4	
5	

Chapter 3: Places

On the following pages you can write about where your ancestors lived. You can mention, for example, local historical events, natural disasters, politics, landscape features, any name changes of the city/town, and anything else that may provide insight into your ancestors' lives.

Place:

Place:

Place:

Place:

Place:

Place:

Place:

Place:

Place:

Place:

Place:

Place:

Place:

Place:

Chapter 4: Places of worship

Here you can write about the places of worship where your ancestors were, for example, christened, married or buried, as well as their history, registers, and contact information.

Place of worship:

Place of worship:

Place of worship:

Place of worship:

Place of worship:

Place of worship:

Place of worship:

Place of worship:

Place of worship:

Place of worship:

Place of worship:

Place of worship:

Place of worship:

Place of worship:

Chapter 5: General notes

These pages can be used for general notes about the genealogical research.

Notes

Notes

Notes

Notes

Notes

Notes

Notes

Notes

Notes

Chapter 6: Genealogical table (Ahnentafel)

In this chapter you can make a genealogical table for both the maternal and the paternal side of the family, using the so-called ahnentafel.
An ahnentafel (German for "genealogical table") is a numbering system for listing a person's direct ancestors in a fixed sequence of ascent.

- Every person listed in the genealogical table has a unique number.

- Apart from No. 1, who can be male or female, all even-numbered individuals are male, and all odd-numbered individuals are female.

- The number of any person's father is double that person's number.
  For instance:
  Paternal side: Father = 2, grandfather = 4, great-grandfather = 8
  Maternal side: Mother = 3, grandfather = 6, great-grandfather = 12

  The number of any person's mother is double that person's number plus one.
  For instance:
  Paternal side: Grandmother = 5, great-grandmother = 11 (2 x 5 +1)
  Maternal side: Mother = 3, grandmother = 7 (2 x 3 + 1), great-grandmother = 15 (2 x 7 + 1)

In the last column of each page you can write the page number of the person's data sheet in Chapter 1.

Genealogical table (Ahnentafel)

First generation

1	You		Page:

Second generation: Parents

2	Father		Page:
3	Mother		Page:

Third generation: Grandparents

4	Father's father		Page:
5	Father's mother		Page:

6	Mother's father		Page:
7	Mother's mother		Page:

Fourth generation: Great-grandparents

8	Father's father's father		Page:
9	Father's father's mother		Page:

10	Father's mother's father		Page:
11	Father's mother's mother		Page:

12	Mother's father's father		Page:
13	Mother's father's mother		Page:

14	Mother's mother's father		Page:
15	Mother's mother's mother		Page:

Fifth generation: Great-great-grandparents

16	Father's father's father's father		Page:
17	Father's father's father's mother		Page:

18	Father's father's mother's father		Page:
19	Father's father's mother's mother		Page:

20	Father's mother's father's father		Page:
21	Father's mother's father's mother		Page:

22	Father's mother's mother's father		Page:
23	Father's mother's mother's mother		Page:

24	Mother's father's father's father		Page:
25	Mother's father's father's mother		Page:

26	Mother's father's mother's father		Page:
27	Mother's father's mother's mother		Page:

28	Mother's mother's father's father		Page:
29	Mother's mother's father's mother		Page:

30	Mother's mother's mother's father		Page:
31	Mother's mother's mother's mother		Page:

Sixth generation: Great-great-great-grandparents

32	Father's father's father's father's father		Page:
33	Father's father's father's fathers mother		Page:

34	Father's father's father's mother's father		Page:
35	Father's father's father's mother's mother		Page:

36	Father's father's mother's father's father		Page:
37	Father's father's mother's father's mother		Page:

38	Father's father's mother's mother's father		Page:
39	Father's father's mother's mother's mother		Page:

40	Father's mother's father's father's father		Page:
41	Father's mother's father's father's mother		Page:

42	Father's mother's father's mother's father		Page:
43	Father's mother's father's mother's mother		Page:

44	Father's mother's mother's father's father		Page:
45	Father's mother's mother's father's mother		Page:

46	Father's mother's mother's mother's father		Page:
47	Father's mother's mother's mother's mother		Page:

Sixth generation: Great-great-great-grandparents

48	Mother's father's father's father's father		Page:
49	Mother's father's father's father's mother		Page:

50	Mother's father's father's mother's father		Page:
51	Mother's father's father's mother's mother		Page:

52	Mother's father's mother's father's father		Page:
53	Mother's father's mother's father's mother		Page:

54	Mother's father's mother's mother's father		Page:
55	Mother's father's mother's mother's mother		Page:

56	Mother's mother's father's father's father		Page:
57	Mother's mother's father's father's mother		Page:

58	Mother's mother's father's mother's father		Page:
59	Mother's mother's father's mother's mother		Page:

60	Mother's mother's mother's father's father		Page:
61	Mother's mother's mother's father's mother		Page:

62	Mother's mother's mother's mother's father		Page:
63	Mother's mother's mother's mother's mother		Page:

Seventh generation: Great-great-great-great-grandparents

64	Father's father's father's father's father's father		Page:
65	Father's father's father's father's father's mother		Page:

66	Father's father's father's father's mother's father		Page:
67	Father's father's father's father's mother's mother		Page:

68	Father's father's father's mother's father's father		Page:
69	Father's father's father's mother's father's mother		Page:

70	Father's father's father's mother's mother's father		Page:
71	Father's father's father's mother's mother's mother		Page:

72	Father's father's mother's father's father's father		Page:
73	Father's father's mother's father's father's mother		Page:

74	Father's father's mother's father's mother's father		Page:
75	Father's father's mother's father's mother's mother		Page:

76	Father's father's mother's mother's father's father		Page:
77	Father's father's mother's mother's father's mother		Page:

78	Father's father's mother's mother's mother's father		Page:
79	Father's father's mother's mother's mother's mother		Page:

80	Father's mother's father's father's father's father		Page:
81	Father's mother's father's father's father's mother		Page:

Seventh generation: Great-great-great-great-grandparents

82	Father's mother's father's father's mother's father		Page:
83	Father's mother's father's father's mother's mother		Page:

84	Father's mother's father's mother's father's father		Page:
85	Father's mother's father's mother's father's mother		Page:

86	Father's mother's father's mother's mother's father		Page:
87	Father's mother's father's mother's mother's mother		Page:

88	Father's mother's mother's father's father's father		Page:
89	Father's mother's mother's father's father's mother		Page:

90	Father's mother's mother's father's mother's father		Page:
91	Father's mother's mother's father's mother's mother		Page:

92	Father's mother's mother's mother's father's father		Page:
93	Father's mother's mother's mother's father's mother		Page:

94	Father's mother's mother's mother's mother's father		Page:
95	Father's mother's mother's mother's mother's mother		Page:

96	Mother's father's father's father's father's father		Page:
97	Mother's father's father's father's father's mother		Page:

98	Mother's father's father's father's mother's father		Page:
99	Mother's father's father's father's mother's mother		Page:

Seventh generation: Great-great-great-great-grandparents

100	Mother's father's father's mother's father's father		Page:
101	Mother's father's father's mother's father's mother		Page:

102	Mother's father's father's mother's mother's father		Page:
103	Mother's father's father's mother's mother's mother		Page:

104	Mother's father's mother's father's father's father		Page:
105	Mother's father's mother's father's father's mother		Page:

106	Mother's father's mother's father's mother's father		Page:
107	Mother's father's mother's father's mother's mother		Page:

108	Mother's father's mother's mother's father's father		Page:
109	Mother's father's mother's mother's father's mother		Page:

110	Mother's father's mother's mother's mother's father		Page:
111	Mother's father's mother's mother's mother's mother		Page:

112	Mother's mother's father's father's father's father		Page:
113	Mother's mother's father's father's father's mother		Page:

114	Mother's mother's father's father's mother's father		Page:
115	Mother's mother's father's father's mother's mother		Page:

116	Mother's mother's father's mother's father's father		Page:
117	Mother's mother's father's mother's father's mother		Page:

Seventh generation: great-great-great-great-grandparents

118	Mother's mother's father's mother's mother's father		Page:
119	Mother's mother's father's mother's mother's mother		Page:

120	Mother's mother's mother's father's father's father		Page:
121	Mother's mother's mother's father's father's mother		Page:

122	Mother's mother's mother's father's mother's father		Page:
123	Mother's mother's mother's father's mother's mother		Page:

124	Mother's mother's mother's mother's father's father		Page:
125	Mother's mother's mother's mother's father's mother		Page:

126	Mother's mother's mother's mother's mother's father		Page:
127	Mother's mother's mother's mother's mother's mother		Page:

Notes

Chapter 7: Research log

Here you can write a summary of your findings, questions, list of sources you have already searched or plan to search, comments about your search strategies, analyses and discrepancies, suggestions and correspondence.

Research log

Research log

Research log

ововс
Research log

Research log

Research log

Research log

Research log

Chapter 8: To-do list

It's easy to become overwhelmed by the quantity of tasks for your research. Organizing your tasks into a to-do list can make everything much more manageable. On the next pages you can make a list of your tasks, mentioning for example websites you would like to check, images you want to download, passengers lists you're looking for, archives you have to contact, family members you'd like to interview.

To do

To do

To do

To do

To do

To do

To do

Chapter 9: Archives & Genealogical organizations

Here you can record the contact information of relevant archives and genealogical organizations.

Archives

Name	Address	Website

Archives

Name	Address	Website

Archives

Name	Address	Website

Archives

Name	Address	Website

Archives

Name	Address	Website

Archives

Name	Address	Website

Archives

Name	Address	Website

Chapter 10: File index

During your research you will probably collect a lot of items, such as photocopies of old documents, photographs of ancestors, correspondence with archives, and maps. You might save some items in a drawer, others in a box or binder. You might save information regarding two generations or regarding seven generations.
No matter how much information you save, you might feel the need to have some kind of overview to organize your items.
Instead of making a highly organized personal archive, you can easily keep track of your items by filling in the lists in this chapter. In the left-hand column you write down which item you saved (photograph, letter, scan etc.) and in the right-hand column you write down where you stored it, such as in a binder, drawer, box or even a computer file.

Files

What	Stored in

Files

What	Stored in

Files

What	Stored in

Files

What	Stored in

Files

What	Stored in

Chapter 11: Index of ancestors' names

Chapter 1 contains the 127 ancestors' data sheets. Here you can list all of the ancestors mentioned in Chapter 1 and the page number of each ancestor's data sheet.

Persons

Full name:	Date of birth	Page

Persons

Full name:	Date of birth	Page

Persons

Full name:	Date of birth	Page

Persons

Full name:	Date of birth	Page

Persons

Full name:	Date of birth	Page

Persons

Full name:	Date of birth	Page

Made in the
USA
Middletown, DE